Musical Thought in Ancient Greece

Musical Thought in Ancient Greece

Edward A. Lippman

COLUMBIA UNIVERSITY PRESS

New York and London 1964

Edward A. Lippman is Associate Professor of Music at Columbia University.

To Vi, Bob, and Richard

Prefatory Note

I would like to express my gratitude to the Guggenheim Foundation, which awarded me a fellowship in the history of musical philosophy and aesthetics for the 1958–59 academic year, and to the Columbia University Council for Research in the Humanities, for a grant I received in the summer of 1960. Particular thanks are due to Marjorie Nicolson, for her helpful suggestions and her unfailing encouragement. This book is part of a larger plan in which additional volumes will carry the history up to the twentieth century.

EDWARD A. LIPPMAN

Columbia University in the City of New York
June, 1964

Contents

Introduction

The historian of musical thought does not deal with a continuous and clearly marked out body of source material, but is confronted instead with a bewildering diversity of ideas. There are musical views in every conceivable kind of document: in metaphysical, scientific, ethical, educational, political, and religious works; in treatises on mathematics, medicine, cosmology, astrology, poetics, rhetoric, architecture, general aesthetics, and musical theory; but rarely in works devoted specifically to a consideration of the nature of music. In addition, there are more popular notions of music in literary works and the writings of musicians: in history, poetry, drama, novels, essays, letters, and criticism. Finally, conceptions of music are implied by musical practice itself: by musical style, instruments, social institutions, kinds of performance and function, and even by scales and notation. Thus the history of musical thought coincides in part with numberless branches of historical study, including those more general disciplines such as cultural history, the history of philosophy, and intellectual history, which make a contribution to the work of every specialized historian.

This complex state of affairs is undoubtedly due to the peculiarities of music itself; existing in intimate relationship with almost every aspect of human activity, music could hardly give rise to an isolated or well-defined area of thought. As a result, the greatest difficulties threaten the historian with defeat, but at the same time, his undertaking is justified and even demanded as a distinct department of historical investigation, since the province of music is not only vast but unique. Conceptions of music could otherwise not be encompassed by any specialized division of historical study, but only by a universal history, where they could not conceivably receive adequate treatment.

It is valuable also to consider the relation of various nonhistorical disciplines to our subject, for we necessarily examine history from a particular vantage point determined by our own historical position and by various analytic and systematic ideas. Thus the natural sciences will provide us with insight into the physical and physiological nature of music, while musical theory and psychology and philosophy will furnish concepts of musical structure and significance. Yet strictly speaking, it is only musical acoustics and physiology which can seriously claim to be nonhistorical in nature, and even here, although this may be true of auditory physiology or of the transmission of sound, for example, it is scarcely equally true of vocal physiology or of architectural acoustics or of systems of temperament or of the construction of instruments. At any rate, in these latter divisions of science, we apply our analyses to vastly different material according to the kind of music we examine, and the abstract general theory is of little interest.

In the case of musical theory and psychology and philosophy, it is highly questionable whether we can develop a general analysis at all, or whether any concept of musical structure or musical perception or the nature of music will cast light over more than a restricted historical area. Truly nonhistorical qualities of musical apprehension and truly universal descriptions of the nature of music appear to be limited to the most elementary facts. Beyond the description given by natural science, which changes only in the course of physical and biological evolution, musical experience is a historical variable. Ultimately this turns musical theory and psychology and philosophy into historical studies, into particular investigations of the music and ideas of past or present, or systematic inventories of the human possibilities uncovered during the history of society and culture. It also produces the most intimate relationship between the philosophy of music and the history of musical conceptions.

If our own philosophy of music is truly to reflect present-day historical awareness, and if it is to succeed to the largest generality possible to it while avoiding the most common mistake of the past—which was to assume the universal validity of conceptions based on limited knowledge and experience—it must make full use of both the history of music and the history of musical thought.

Musical Thought in Ancient Greece

I. Conceptions of Harmony

That the world is characterized by ordered structure is a feeling apparently shared by all higher cultures; and in any particular instance, the way in which this feeling is expressed, the kind of beliefs to which it gives rise, must constitute a feature of the culture which is important and distinctive, if only because it is so fundamental. In ancient Greece, the notion of natural order was shaped by thought of such vigor and universality that there could be no question of confining it within the bounds of natural philosophy; it came to be vitally important also to conceptions of man and society and art. It is doubtless because of the commanding position held by this idea that the constitution of works of art or of society was seen less as a contrivance of man than as a reflection of nature, and many aesthetic problems never came into the focus of attention.

But the reverse process (which is foreshadowed in animism and myth) was important too: the natural world was viewed in terms of life and mind, its order testified to plan and reason and divinity or to the idea of organic wholeness that is embodied in the concept of cosmos. Thus the interrelation of man and the world brought ideas of natural order into the human province and infused ethical and religious and aesthetic values into the sphere of nature. In addition, this generalized order was distinguished by a musical character, and was typically thought of as harmonic. Why this was so or how it came about is not easy to determine, but strangely enough, synesthetic and mythical factors involving actual sonority do not seem to play a major role, for the harmony of the world is a rational and abstract property that is different in principle from any concrete manifestation to sense.

Yet harmony does not necessarily involve either number or measurement. It means simply "fitting together," as manifested typically in carpentry in the joining of two pieces of wood, and the basic prerequisite of the conception is thus the existence of two or more distinguishable entities somehow capable of mutual adjustment. From the beginning the idea was connected with music.

The process of fitting together is peculiarly applicable to spatial or simultaneous constituents, and Greek music was in essence purely melodic; but in the tuning of the lyre there existed a simultaneity that was possibly not just an example but the true model of the whole conception. Given a world replete with internal relationships, music can easily account not only for the mathematical meanings of harmony, but for the entire generality of the term which develops as part of a progressive musicalization of every aspect of experience. For music conspicuously contains the factor of agreeable sensation; it is based on the internal adjustment of the opposites high and low; and it presents that complex example of fitting together which is manifested in the *harmonia* or musical system of the octave.

The consonance of the octave itself was also known as *harmonia,* as we can see in the musical discussion of harmony by Philolaus;[1] it was a harmony not only of two tones which are at once opposed and similar, but also of two consonances—the fourth and fifth—which are different rather than opposite, but which even more graphically "fit together" to make an octave. It is the peculiarity of the conception of harmony to unite this specifically musical character with the apparently contradictory feature of abstract generality, and the puzzle is compounded by the fact that a simultaneous relationship was attached to a temporal art. When "harmony" came to designate the chordal aspect of music, there occurred something like a historical solution of a paradox.

In any event, music reveals the complex mathematical order of the tonal system precisely in its connection with and dependence upon the more elementary duality of high and low, as well as providing this duality itself with a rational basis in the proportions of consonance. At the same time, it is related more intimately and pervasively with the physical and visual world through the tensions of stringed instruments and the dimensions of musical instruments of all types. Finally, in its temporal character it is able to bring the whole class of cyclic events under the head of harmony, which as a notion of fitting together might otherwise have remained limited for the most part to simultaneous phenomena. It is obvious that music was strategically situated to lend elaboration and structure to the concept of harmony in a way that proved ineradicable. Indeed the term "music" becomes at times more or less synonymous with "harmony," and takes on the same breadth of meaning. But this inherent suitability of music to its task had to await discovery and use by a culture that found it to be a natural expression of its outlook.

Etymology emphasizes the generality of the field of conceptions to which harmony belongs.[2] *Ar* or *har* enters a great variety of verbs in the Indo-European languages, signifying the unification of disparate or conflicting elements into an ordered whole. Verbs in early Greek literature beginning with this etymon have a broad range of application, and encompass not only the performance of music and the tuning of an instrument, but a physical binding together and a mental pacification, a transitive fitting together and an intransitive adaptation. Greek gives full representation to the physical and logical spheres of the Indo-European prefix, but neglects the temporal one completely for centuries. Homer uses *ararisko* "connect," *aresko* "adapt, reconcile, satisfy," *arasso* "slam together, strike, play the lyre," and *harmozo* "fit together." The last verb has a purely physical meaning in Homer, with a much more restricted application than the noun *harmonia,* but in later times it exceeded the noun in the versatility and breadth of its use, encompassing the diversity of "marry, arrange, administer, tune, kiss" which is revealed in Pindar, Herodotus, Plato, Aristophanes, and Euripides. *Harmonia* developed its variety of meaning earlier, and already designates in Homer not only a physical "connecting link" but a mental and qualitative "agreement."

2. Duality is a universal motif of myth; in Greece, the duality issues

OVER

in harmony, which is revealed as the outcome of opposed but recon-
ciled forces. The Boeotian myth makes Harmonia the daughter of
Ares, the god of war, and Aphrodite, the goddess of love and beauty,
while the Attic version develops the musical element: Harmonia is
not only the daughter of Zeus and the Atlantide Elektra, but she is
also the mother of the Muses.

Paired opposites remain as fundamental to scientific cosmogony as
they are to theogony and myth. Thus a path is provided along
which harmony enters into philosophic thought. But the importance
of the cosmological role of harmony is guaranteed by additional
factors that lend themselves readily to harmonic treatment: the motions of the heavens, the cycle of the seasons, and the idea of primary
physical materials or elements. If we examine them closely, however,
we find that these factors are all related. At first the elements are
thought of not so much as general constituents, but as large masses
which have particular locations in the world, and which may come
into existence successively, like the divinities in a theogony. Earth is
typically surrounded by concentric spheres of water, air, and fire, for
example, or one of the elements will be treated as the source of the
others. Thus the relationship between the spheres can become a
basis for the relationship between the elements, while on the other
hand the elements themselves can be reduced to more fundamental
qualitative opposites, such as hot and cold, and wet and dry. Again,
these are not only general forces, but can succeed one another in a
seasonal cycle. Often qualities are not distinguished from elements;
the quality "hot," for example, will be identical with the object
"fire," rather than one of its components. Traces of such an origin
are preserved in the tendency of elements—even in the classical
system of Empedocles—to fall into pairs of contraries. The most
conspicuous natural foundations of this whole pattern of thought—
and the closest to myth—are the polarities of heaven and earth, male
and female, and day and night. And at the other extreme stand the
ultimate philosophic versions of duality: the abstract opposites

sameness and otherness, or the limited and the unlimited, which are capable of serving in the generation of number or of the soul.

The history of harmony, however, is by no means coincident with the history of elements and opposites, or even with the history of the basic concept of cosmos. Only in particular schools of thought are cosmogonic processes and cosmic structures regarded as specifically harmonic, although in other cases we are often confronted with descriptions that are in fact if not in name essentially those of harmony. In the course of time, words such as *isonomia* are replaced by *harmonia,* while other concepts, such as those of mixture and measure and proportion, become charged with a musical significance. To explain the expansion and success of the concept of harmony we must identify the way in which it differs from other notions of order. Its distinctive feature is its aesthetic connotation, in particular its rich musical values, and their emotional and structural appropriateness to their task.

Early Ionian cosmology is too imperfectly preserved for us to determine the precise nature of its theories.[3] That it was to some extent harmonic in conception, however, is suggested by its systematic and geometrical nature, and also by the fact that it was the central source of later Greek ideas. Anaximander, the most important of the natural philosophers of Ionia in the sixth century B.C., described the birth of paired contraries from the boundless apeiron. Cosmic process was legal rather than harmonic: a divine justice controlled coming to be and passing away, exacting retribution for the illegal excesses of cold and hot, and wet and dry. The sun, the moon, and the stars were three wheels filled with fire and spaced according to mathematical proportions, very much as in later systems of cosmic harmony.

In the latter part of the sixth century, as a result of the Persian conquest of the Greek cities of Asia Minor, Ionia gave way to southern Italy as the main seat of philosophic thought, and various natively Ionian philosophers migrated to this new location, where, at Croton and in other Italian cities, the Pythagorean school was the first to achieve prominence.[4] According to tradition from Herodotus to Iamblichus, Pythagoras of Samos acquired both his mystical and mathematical wisdom from Babylonian and Egyptian sources, during an extended period of foreign travel, and there can be little doubt that the foundations of both his religious code and his scientific theory must be sought in these ancient Mediterranean civilizations as well as in Orphism.

But as difficult as it is to specify the older constituents of Pythagorean thought, it is still more difficult to determine the precise achievements of Pythagoras himself. We may safely say, however, that no one in Western musical philosophy has had an influence equally powerful. With the early Pythagoreans, active toward the end of the sixth century, the notion of harmony acquired its epochal connection with mathematics, and also its more specifically musical character. They imparted to Greek and to European thought a lasting prejudice that tied music to the cosmos, to rational order, and to ethical value as well, and these ties dominated the musical outlook of both antiquity and the Middle Ages.

Although philosophy was typically a way of life in ancient times, it was especially so for the Pythagoreans. The movement was primarily religious, social, and political, and perhaps the true greatness of its founder was that of providing inspiration and leadership. The brotherhood practiced a type of Orphic religion characterized by an elaborate doctrine and an associated rule of behavior; the code was severe, and involved taboos, discipline, and asceticism. A central doctrine was the immortality and transmigration of the soul, which could travel from human to animal; that abstinence from meat was enjoined may very well have been a consequence. The silence kept by the Pythagoreans may have been disciplinary rather than secretive, but whatever the reason, much of their belief and practice remained unknown to outsiders. Certainly their chief concern was with purification, but this is no more than a corollary of their conception of the soul.

Joined to this basic religious outlook and not merely existing side-by-side with it was a profound interest in mathematics and in a metaphysics founded on mathematics. The significant association of religion and mathematical speculation created a fostering climate for a powerful and purely theoretic interest in science, which in its religious motivation and freedom from practical concerns could easily stray into numerology and magic. The theory of numbers and geometry were developed in close association; the proportional theory of vibrating strings was a central scientific discovery; and the Pythagorean cosmogony and cosmology were almost certainly based on a variety of harmonic relationships. That numbers are in some fashion constituents of reality was the fundamental metaphysical notion of the Pythagoreans. End

Unfortunately it is impossible to determine the precise form of this belief; whether all things were held to be numbers literally, or simply to be numerical in their form and properties, we do not know, but in either case the conception remains important and fruitful. It can be understood only by keeping in mind the fact that number was represented in concrete physical form: by geometrical figures, by arrays of ciphers, and notably by the arrangement of pebbles. Thus number was not readily abstracted from physical reality as it is in more modern thought, and although representation by groups of counters may belong to calculation and elementary pedagogy rather than to the science of arithmetic, it was undoubtedly also suggestive for the philosophy and theory of numbers. But a concrete conception of number obviously contained two inherent difficulties: zero could not exist, and incommensurable physical and geometrical magnitudes had a peculiar "irrational" status. Prime numbers were arranged in rows, and those with two and three factors, in various plane and solid figures according to their properties. Another restriction here was the impossibility of exceeding three dimensions.

The most important of the Pythagorean numbers was the tetractys of the decad, a quaternary consisting of the first four integers. This was sacred; it yielded the perfect number *10,* and thus provided the underlying reason for the decimal basis of counting. It had a musical implication in that all sets of four were regarded as somehow harmonious and controlled in the relationship of their elements, and more specifically in that it furnished the ratios for the basic consonances of octave, double-octave, twelfth, fifth, and fourth (2:1 4:1, 3:1, 3:2, and 4:3).

Also of great importance musically was the theory of means and proportion. The early Pythagoreans knew that the musical consonances involved the subcontrary as well as the arithmetic and geometric relationships, and the subcontrary mean was named "harmonic," possibly by Hippasus. Specifically, string lengths arranged in the pattern 12,9,8,6 gave the intervals of fourth, fifth, and octave, so that the consonances which were the framework of the scale could be derived from the arithmetic and harmonic means between two quantities in the ratio 2:1.

The early Pythagoreans doubtless found consonant relationships in the macroscopic structure of the world also, and they may have thought of cosmic harmony as in some sense actually sounding, although it is possible that they would not have seen any importance or even any meaning in such a question. The suggestiveness of acoustic phenomena was undoubtedly very great; like rows of pebbles, strings present numbers as lengths, and they make their properties audible as well as visible and tangible. Most important, however, is the easily discovered fact that consonances, and therefore numerical properties, do not reside only in relationships of length. Strings differing in tension or in physical qualities contain harmony in a much more mysterious way, and tend to suggest that number is of the essence of reality even when it is imperceptible.

The diverse factors of the Pythagorean outlook seem originally to

have been part of a unified picture provided by an important cosmogonic theory, which can be reconstructed hypothetically in outline
from later reports.[5] The fundamental principles were the paired
contraries, the limited and the unlimited. From these, number was
generated, *1* representing their initial combination and containing
in itself, as a result, both the odd and the even. A second similar
process gave rise to 2, and successive repetitions to *3* and *4*. This
constituted the tetractys of the decad; after *10* the series simply
repeated itself.

Numbers gave rise to geometric figures: a second unit placed
alongside the first generated a line from a point, a third unit placed so
as to form a triangle produced the basic two-dimensional figure, and
a fourth unit placed on top of these made a tetrahedron, the first
three-dimensional figure. Thus geometry, too, was derived from the
tetractys. And from geometry the physical world was generated, for
the tetrahedron, the basic sold form, became the physical element
fire, which was situated in the center of the world and drew upon
the unlimited surrounding it to complete the cosmogonical process.
The crucial point, the relationship between the mathematical and
physical entities, we are unable to determine; we do not know
whether mathematics was conceived as giving the form of the physical world, in which case there would be a true problem of genesis,
or whether the two were identified, so that the tetrahedron and fire
were one and the same. And this ambiguity arises again in the relationship of arithmetic and geometry; as we have indicated, a genesis
of figures from pebble-like material constituents is certainly unable
to account for incommensurable lengths. The closest view we can
secure is given by the cosmogony of Plato's *Timaeus,* a monument
to the human imagination which is undoubtedly an elaboration of
the Pythagorean tradition and which strongly emphasizes the harmonic nature of the cosmos, although it does not entirely remove
the enigma surrounding the issues we have mentioned.

A conception of harmony very different from those of the early

Pythagoreans, but equally profound, was advanced by Heraclitus of Ephesus,[6] active around 500 B.C. Heraclitus finds certainty in self-knowledge rather than in the examination of nature and the amassing of learning. His combination of reason with the empiricism of the Ionians appears to anticipate Plato; but Heraclitus does not believe in changeless ideal entities behind perceptible phenomena; the interrelation is more intimate, and indeed his dynamic conception of harmony was easily misunderstood. The critique offered by Eryximachus in Plato's *Symposium*[7] conspicuously fails to do it justice, Plato depicting the physician as hopelessly misled by Heraclitean paradox. Love and harmony both present the same problem: are their constituents opposite or similar? or are they necessarily related in any way even before their harmonization?

In other dialogues of Plato also, considerable complication arises over the relationship of contraries; those of the phenomenal world flow into one another and only in the world of forms are opposites irrevocably distinct. But this kind of machinery is not necessary to Heraclitus, for his picture of the world is only superficially similar to Plato's, and is not actually dualistic at all. The universe is one of ceaseless change, but it contains a harmony that controls both spatial and temporal phenomena. Enmeshed in the process of the world, hidden somehow in the very midst of the change and transience typified in fire, is a divine Logos, a measure and proportion. The river is constant change, but it is permanence as well; it is always the same river, and by measure, the arrival of water is balanced with its passage at any point.

This element of regulation and order in the world is not found simply in external nature nor is it simply subjective; indeed this distinction has no importance, and the order is as omnipresent as the change: it is at once cosmic and ethical. Harmony is perhaps a more adequate description of its nature than either measure or logos, for harmony shows the inevitable relation to opposites, the holding in balance of forces at odds with one another; in a word, the central connection of permanence with transience. We can come to know the divine order of harmony more readily in ourselves than in the external world, and it is the knowledge of this universal but secret logos that gives Heraclitus his superior and cryptic manner and his scorn for the rest of mankind, philosophers included. On the other hand, the very nature of his conception of harmony accounts for the paradox and enigma in the writings of "the dark one." This hidden harmony is more important than any known by the senses, for without it the world would fall to pieces. Yet conflict and opposition are also essential everywhere; they can be called not prerequisites but corequisites.

But things at variance really agree; unity is bestowed by harmony, or if we wish, harmony is really unity. Significantly, it is a musical instrument, the lyre, that Heraclitus uses, along with the bow, to exemplify his conception. In both, opposed forces are connected with one another and adjusted, while from a dynamic point of view, when the strings are drawn back, the restoration of harmony produces music in the one case and marksmanship in the other—parallel and really equivalent manifestations, for both overcome distance, whether with sound or arrow, to reach their target, both are outcomes of action that is at the same time harmonious and accurately directed, and both are symbols of a life correctly lived so as to achieve its goal. Even literally, whether in instrument or in weapon, music and accuracy are present together, for the bow is not silent in action, and like the flight of sound, the arrow is audible in travel. The depth of the concept reaches back to the identification of musical bow and hunting bow in prehistory. In addition, although its work is death, the bow (*biós*) is life (*bíos*); and in this we have a Greek example of the metaphysical significance found in sonorous resemblance. Temporal events, too, reveal the same principles; night is succeeded by day, winter by summer, and every aspect of the world has its opposite, even where we do not perceive it. A comprehensive concept of harmony is consequently a central feature of Heraclitus' philosophy.

The Eleatic school, which developed in the first half of the fifth century and is represented mainly by Parmenides,[8] had its basis in reason rather than sensory experience or number, and produced a strict ontology grounded on logic. While the indivisibility and immutability that it deduced as the properties of Being left no room for harmony, Parmenides recognized in addition to a changeless reality, a world of sense and seeming, for which the question of cosmogony again became meaningful. Here were to be found sensible contraries, such as light and darkness, and hot and cold, along with a guiding goddess of harmony who ruled over the union of male and female, and who devised a theogony starting with the creation of Eros. But Parmenides took an extreme stand with respect to the relation of truth and appearance; he saw no point of contact between them, and both this separation and his emphasis on the superior reality of Being were obviously of great importance in the constitution of Plato's metaphysics.

The Sicilian philosopher Empedocles,[9] who flourished about 450 B.C. and who resembles Pythagoras in combining science with a cult of purification, established the canonical system of four elements, or "roots" (rhizomata): earth, water, air, fire; and of two cosmic forces that act on them: love and strife. Everything in the world is a mixture of the elements harmonized by Aphrodite. When constituents are most similar, harmony and love are strongest, and this is particularly the case in the connection of earth, sea, heaven, and sun with their own parts. Generation and destruction also, after Parmenides, could be conceived only as a mixture and separation, but they are controlled by the dominance of love and hate respectively. Empedocles' cosmogony, in which elements and forces are still identified with divinity, is thus conceived as a harmonic process, and the distinguishing feature of his conception of harmony is its dependence on the similarity of the harmonized constituents. This is a characteristic that undoubtedly is due to his emphasis on the role of love. There is also an alternation of love and hate; in turn the elements unite to form a unity and separate to form a multiplicity; but this oscillation does not seem to have been thought of as a temporal version of harmony.

The later Ionian philosopher Anaxagoras of Clazomenae,[10] whose writings come somewhat after those of Empedocles and who is important in having made Athens the center of his philosophic activity, was the originator of the important concept of Nous, or mind, as an ordering force in the world. As Anaxagoras conceived it, however, Nous was not immaterial, but rather a distinctively tenuous and pure kind of matter. Both in its nature and its function, it was thus a logical successor of the Heraclitean Logos, the divine fire. Like the love and strife of Empedocles, Nous in effect produced an analysis of the hylozoistic idea of primitive material, extracting the causal components of force and motion and life, and leaving an inert matter conceived in the form of basic qualitative elements, or "seeds" (*spermata*). Sensible things and even the elements of Empedocles became harmonic mixtures of these seeds produced by the action of Nous and then by a resultant series of mechanical events. One type of seed predominates in each mixture and is responsible for the quality of the whole.

Towards 400 B.C., about a century after the time of Pythagoras, we come upon the first of the later Pythagoreans whose ideas have been preserved in some detail. Nicomachus tells us that Philolaus demonstrated harmonic proportion by making use of the cube, which has twelve edges, eight vertices, and six faces.[11] And the Philolaic fragments testify to an interest in harmony that is both ramified and deep.[12]

Philolaus calls the octave *harmonia,* describes it as containing the fifth and the fourth, and gives the ratios of all three intervals; he also defines the tone as the difference between fifth and fourth, so that its ratio becomes 9:8, and considers the system of the octave as filled in with such tones—of which the fourth contains two and the fifth three—plus the two remaining semitonal intervals. This gives the basic theoretical pattern underlying the scales and modes of Greek music; if the fourth is placed above the fifth and the tones inserted in each case with the semitonal remainder at the bottom, the result is a Dorian scale of the diatonic genus.

Philolaus also deals with the metaphysical nature of harmony. He advances the concept that the world and everything in it are made up of two kinds of elements, the limiting and the boundless. These two fundamental elements or principles are seen to be structurally insufficient, however, for they are unequal and unrelated; harmony is also required. Here we learn the vitally important fact that the Pythagorean contraries were combined by a harmonic process. As far as number is concerned, Philolaus holds that it brings things into agreement with perception and makes them cognizable and capable of interrelationship, while without it they would not be clear either in themselves or in relation to one another.

Thus number belongs to everything that can be known; its very nature is such as to give knowledge. Like knowledge, truth is inherent in number and specific to it, while falsehood is hostile to number and irreconcilable with it, belonging instead to the nature of the boundless, the senseless, and the unreasonable. Philolaus stresses the universality of number: it plays a role everywhere—not only in divine things but in all human works and words, including music. But if the fragments give number an epistemological function, they give harmony an ontologic one, and reveal it not only as a product of number, but also as its foundation.

Although he may not have devised it himself, Philolaus transmitted what was widely accepted as the standard Pythagorean cosmology, but unfortunately we have no information about the mathematical details of its structure. An important feature of the system is that the earth is not placed at the center of the universe; this position is occupied by a central fire which is surrounded by ten wheels bearing successively a counter-earth, the earth, the sun, the moon, the five planets, and the fixed stars. Aristotle believed that the counter-earth had been introduced solely to bring the number of wheels to ten; that is, as a manifestation of the holy tetractys, but it could just as well have been invented to account for eclipses. On the other hand, the number *10* has been taken to exclude the possibility that harmonic notions were part of the Philolaic cosmology, since there were only seven tones in the Greek scale. The earliest Greek systems of planetary harmony that have come down to us, however, reveal a concern with consonances rather than with the scale, and the number of wheels is determined by other factors. This by no means proves that Aristotle was right in his explanation of the ten wheels, but he certainly might have been, and in any event, it is difficult to believe that Pythagorean astronomy could have been unrelated to harmony. The musical cosmology of Plato's *Timaeus,* which is expounded in the dialogue by a Pythagorean, is almost proof of the point, although we really do not have sufficient evidence to establish the matter either way.

Of Eurytus,[13] who was active in southern Italy around 400 B.C., we have only Aristotle's report that he decided what was the number of what—of man or of horse—by imitating the figures of living things with pebbles, as some people bring numbers into the forms of triangle and square. But about Archytas of Tarentum, a pupil of Philolaus and a friend of Plato, we are again considerably better informed.[14] He concerned himself with the traditional group of Pythagorean studies that later became the quadrivium, discussing the kinship of geometry, arithmetic, astronomy, and music, which he mentions in this order; he admires the work of mathematicians in these disciplines, and especially in music. The studies are *mathemata;* they are all related because they deal with the two primary forms of being, by which he presumably means multitude and extension. Music, here identical with harmonics, is thus explicitly rec-

ognized as one of the mathematical sciences. That Archytas wrote
on all of these sciences himself is more than likely; what we know
of his work points in this direction, and the disciplines were so
intimately associated in the Pythagorean outlook that they probably
were always studied together. Indeed Vitruvius mentions Philolaus
and Archytas of Tarentum among the men "on whom nature has
bestowed so much skill, acumen, retentiveness that they can be thoroughly familiar with geometry, astronomy, music and other studies." [15]

In his analysis of the physical nature of sound, Archytas comes
close to the true state of affairs, correctly connecting higher pitch
with speed and power, but he falls into errors of detail by failing to
take vibration or wavelength into account. Ptolemy regards him as
the most important of the Pythagorean writers, and both Ptolemy
and Boethius discuss his calculation of the intervals of the musical
genera, a detailed interest in tuning he might easily have taken over
from his teacher Philolaus. Boethius has also preserved his proof
that no geometric mean exists between two numbers in superparticular ratio, or in terms of integers, between two successive ones, a
theorem which was his central contribution to musical theory, and
which implies specifically that the fifth, the fourth, and the whole
tone cannot be rationally divided into two equal intervals. The proof
is also found considerably later than Archytas in Euclid's *Division
of the Monochord,* or *Section of the Canon* (c.300 B.C.). It has an
additional interest in revealing something of the interconnection of
the mathematical sciences, for it rests on various arithmetical propositions which can be found in Euclid's *Elements* (Book VII); thus
at the same time we learn that the discipline of arithmetic was
known to Archytas in something like the form in which we find it
in Euclid.

Another problem that Archytas solved brilliantly by a three-dimensional construction is that of duplicating the cube, or of finding
two mean proportionals between two straight lines; this theorem

similarly shows the interrelation of the *mathemata,* for it enters into the harmonic cosmogony of Plato's *Timaeus.* More specifically musical is Archytas' discusssion of the arithmetic, geometric, and harmonic means; he defines the three, and considers all to belong to the subject of music, which doubtless signifies that he conceives of this as the general study of relative number, although it is true that the means are all used in the relationships of actual music, so that the mathematical discipline is not so distant from the specific theory of the art. Finally Iamblichus reports that both Philolaus and Archytas were familiar with the "musical" proportion 12,9,8,6, which the Neo-Pythagoreans regarded as the most perfect of all.

The references of Boethius and Ptolemy to Archytas, together with the arithmetical basis of the superparticular proof, make it probable that Archytas ranks with Eudoxus and Theaetetus as one of the most important sources for Euclid's mathematical works. The arithmetical books of the *Elements* (Books VII and VIII in particular) may in large part go back to him, and the Euclid *Section of the Canon* may be essentially a reproduction of his harmonic theory.

Yet Archytas himself admires the work of others in the four mathematical disciplines, and especially in music, so that it is quite likely that harmonics had already achieved an impressive form before his time. Indeed in the first book of his *Harmonics,* Ptolemy gives two Pythagorean systems of the science, and we can with some likelihood take one of these as the work of Archytas (the one that repeats Euclid's *Section of the Canon* and contains the same logical defect) and the other as the work of the Pythagoreans preceding him.

The science of harmonics must have received its theoretical elaboration in the fifth century B.C., in common with the other Pythagorean *mathemata,* and like these, it doubtless was the work of the *mathematikoi,* the scientific division of the brotherhood that had broken away from the religious and secret tenets of the sect in emulation of Hippasus. Harmonics was closely connected with arithmetic in particular; as the sciences of multitude, these were distinguished by limitation to rational quantities. We shall examine harmonics in more detail in Chapter Four, in connection with the Euclid *Section of the Canon.*

It is sufficient to consider here that tone, or more correctly, pitch, was axiomatically connected with number, and consonances with multiple and superparticular ratios. The theorems were concerned with the determination of the ratios that corresponded to the individual consonances and intervals, and as a necessary concomitant, with the compounding and dividing of consonances, a matter doubtless related to the tuning of the lyre. The purely arithmetical theorems were formulated with musical application in mind, and dealt with the geometric mean, which was taken as the equivalent of the bisection of an interval, and with multiple and superparticular ratios. It was shown that if a multiple ratio was compounded the result remained multiple, but that superparticular ratios did not behave in this fashion; 2:1 became 4:1, for example, but 3:2 became 9:4, and left the consonant classes altogether.

Now the evidence of hearing revealed that the doubled octave remained consonant while the doubled fifth or fourth did not, and on this basis it could be demonstrated which ratios corresponded to which intervals. It was also observed that in the arithmetical combination of superparticulars a multiple or superparticular result could be obtained only if the two intervals were different; 3:2 and 4:3 would yield 2:1, for example; and this became the theoretical basis of the musical system; consonances and intervals were divided not in half, or geometrically (which was ruled out on principle whatever the evidence of hearing might be), but arithmetically or harmonically to give all the ratios of the different genera, a method that could supplement or even supplant the somewhat similar device of subtracting one interval or consonance from another. The division of the octave into fifth and fourth became a prototype rather than a unique operation; the major third 5:4 could similarly be divided, for example, to yield the large and small tones 9:8 and 10:9. It seems to have been Archytas who discovered the generality of this principle, which is truly the foundation of harmonics, and he was a pioneer in its systematic application.

By the time of Plato, then, the scientific conception of harmony and music was well established. In the *Theaetetus* [16] we learn that this mathematician and his teacher studied the traditional *mathemata,* and essentially the same group of sciences is discussed in the *Republic* (Book VII), the *Laws* (Book VII), and the *Epinomis.* It might seem that the Sophists would oppose such studies on principle, or at least not find them useful except possibly for purposes of refutation, but even they taught and studied them (although Protagoras was an exception), as we can see in *Protagoras* [17] and in *Lesser Hippias*.[18] More specifically, we are told that under their tutelage pupils reviewed these disciplines or learned them for a second time; mathematics must have been to some extent a general feature of private education, and it was taught in public schools as well, although from a more practical point of view.

Plato's interest in the discipline of harmonics is grounded partly in his conviction that harmony and music have a close relation to the cosmos. One of the ironic etymologies of the *Cratylus* specifically couples music with the harmony of nature.[19] In support of the thesis that the name Apollo means "moving together," Socrates points to the fact that Apollo is the god of harmony; musicians and astronomers both declare that he makes all things move together by a harmonious power, whether in the harmony or concord of song or in the poles of heaven. The discussion links music, prophecy, medicine, and archery, as the four attributes of Apollo, and also points to harmony as the unifying factor, since Apollo is the god of harmony. This suggests not only the Heraclitean coupling of lyre and bow, but also the connection of harmony with wisdom (in the attribute of prophecy) and the concept of medicine as the art of bringing about harmony in body and soul.

The impressively broad scope of the conception of harmony is revealed in the important discourse of the physician Eryximachus in the *Symposium*.[20] The speech is compounded essentially of Hippocratic and Empedoclean theories of the harmony in man and in nature, including the harmony of the seasons, and of wet and dry, and hot and cold. It also contains the criticism of Heraclitus that we have mentioned above, and maintains that harmony is the reconciliation not of opposite elements, but of elements that disagreed once and are now harmonized. Presumably then, harmony is possible only if some alteration in the elements takes place upon harmonization so that they come to possess something in common. If two strings are harmonized, for example, assuming for simplicity that they may differ only in length, we adjust the relationship of the two lengths so that there is a unit by which both strings can be measured. The argument is clearly in line with Empedocles' emphasis on similarity as a prerequisite of harmony. And the fundamental theme of the discourse, the association of harmony and love, also derives from the same philosopher.

Of the most striking expression of the musical constitution of the world, the harmonious properties of the heavens, we really have no clear evidence until the *Republic* and the *Timaeus*. Sensory and synesthetic elements are a distinctive feature of the myth of Er in the *Republic* (Book X); [21] these factors may have been associated with the concepts of the Near East, since Er is described as a native of Pamphylia. The vision of the rotating wheels of the world is a postmortem experience of a warrior killed in battle, who miraculously returns to life to tell his story. The cosmic music actually sounds, and the tones are connected with visual impressions, particularly with colors. Appropriately, the Sirens and not the Muses preside over the music. The intrusion into a cosmological picture of perceptible rather than purely intelligible factors can be explained without great difficulty. It originates doubtless in the fact that to the soul freed from the body, rational apprehension takes on the character of immediate perception. Also the myth of Er is not a straightforward cosmology, but a pedagogical device teaching the ultimate rewards of justice; it is poetry in a more immediate sense than the philosophical dialogue itself, and thus capable of serving a more elementary educational purpose. Accordingly it uses the method of sensory appeal; it is imitative art, but a true imitation.

There are eight wheels in the vision; their appearance is described in respect of the width of their rims, their color, and their speed, but each of the three lists mentions the wheels in a succession that reflects the balanced order underlying them. On each wheel sits a Siren singing one tone, and the eight together form one harmony. In view of the clearly simultaneous nature of the "harmony," it is unlikely that Plato intends to designate a scale. Furthermore a scale is possible, although still unlikely, only if the tones were connected with the widths of the rims of the wheels, or with hypothetical orbital speeds. The angular speeds of the wheels were more or less accurately known, and palpably did not yield a scale. In addition, since three of the angular speeds are given as identical, there could be only six different pitches; a complete scale, at any rate, would be impossible. On the other hand, the radii of the wheels, which are doubtless what the tones represent, were simply not thought of as scalar in their relationship, as we can determine from the account in the *Timaeus*.

To complete the picture of simultaneous harmony, the three Fates join in the singing. They sing of the past, present, and future, thus adding to the music an explicit narration of temporal events. There is a relation between this depiction of time and the time embodied in the rotation of the wheels, for the Fates touch the various wheels at certain intervals and influence their motion: Clotho, who sings of the present, helps with her right hand the revolution of the outer wheel; Atropos, who sings of the future, guides with her left hand the inner wheels, which all revolve slowly but at various speeds in the opposite direction; and Lachesis, who sings of the past, touches first the one and then the other, with each hand in turn. Plato has here provided an ingenious device to "save the appearances" of the complex motions of the stars, and in addition, he makes time subservient to divine control, so that its structure, as revealed in the heavens, becomes significant for human destiny. The Fates represent the connection between human temporal existence and the cosmos, so that the choice of a type of life by each soul, which is described next in the myth, becomes a decision set in the context of cosmic justice.

Quite apart from questions of scientific cosmology, the whole vision is intended to depict justice on a cosmic plane; it is not so much an allegory of justice, but a characteristic union of the cosmological and legal notions in the tradition of Anaximander. Thus each Siren keeps to her own tone, a counterpart in the universe of justice in the state, which consists in each citizen doing his own business. And this in turn is a parallel of justice within the individual. Appropriately reflecting the concept of justice, the array of relationships in the cosmos is characterized by balance, and this takes on sensible beauty and order for the soul that achieves a vantage point giving direct insight. Injustice is then seen to be only apparent—a momentary deviation that does not disturb the whole.

The cosmology of the *Timaeus* has a considerably more detailed musical character, and also encompasses the problem of genesis.[22] The cosmos, as a perfect whole of perfect parts, is constructed throughout by a method based on a conception of harmony: intermediates—geometric, arithmetic, and harmonic means—connect its various parts and the opposites it contains. The world is a living organism with a soul as well as a body. Both of these are created by a divine Artificer, a Demiurge who is producing in effect a master work of art, a huge spatial and temporal music. Pythagorean and Ionian traditions are combined in a masterful synthesis that encompasses the mathematical harmonies of the soul and the physical harmonies of the body. The question of the status of number and the Ideas is answered by compounding the soul of their likeness in the form of an impalpable material and its articulations and motions. The soul transcends the body but is intimately connected with it. The Ideas themselves remain without the attribute of location, but the soul explains how they can be relevant to the sensible world and how they can become objects of knowledge. Every constituent of a complete metaphysics is incorporated in a single narrative. Mathematics is divided: number finds its place in the soul and so does the geometry of circles and spheres and rotation; but the rest of geometry—straight lines and all the angular figures—belongs to the physical world as its ultimate basis.

The Artificer first creates the soul of the world, mixing together materials that are related to the general classes of existence as these are described in the late dialogues. The psychogony is based on Pythagorean cosmogonical ideas which Plato transforms and elaborates in conformity with the discoveries of *Parmenides, Sophist,* and *Philebus.* Notions of a harmonic nature are at once involved in the initial process of blending the material of the soul. An intermediate kind of existence is compounded of two contrary constituents—indivisible existence and divisible existence—and this intermediate existence in turn mediates the combination of the opposites sameness and otherness, and is blended with them.

But the harmonic aspect of the world soul is not limited to the constitution of its material, for after this is compounded, it is divided into parts that have the relationships of the tones of a vast Dorian musical scale of the diatonic genus. The range is nearly five octaves—much greater than that of practical Greek music. The structural framework of the scale is a series of increasing magnitudes derived by arranging the terms of two quaternaries in ascending order. These quaternaries—1,2,4,8 and 1,3,9,27—employ the first three powers of 2 and 3 respectively, and have 1 as a common term, so that they can be called a double tetractys. They represent opposites again, this time of odd and even number—a duality which is another version of the contraries sameness and otherness.

Because the soul is tridimensional the series progress to the third power. In each successive interval of this framework two additional portions of the material are placed, equal in size to the arithmetic and harmonic means between the two terms defining the interval. Finally all the resultant musical intervals of a fourth are filled up with whole tones in the ratio 9:8, leaving over in each fourth the diesis 256:243; the product is the Pythagorean diatonic tuning of Philolaus and Archytas.

The scalar series of magnitudes, which we can take as connected one to the other as though they have been marked off along a single strip, is then split lengthwise and formed into two bands, which are bent into circles and arranged like a representation of the celestial equator and the ecliptic. These are set into rotation, the outer motion being called the motion of the same and the inner motion that of the other. Rotation is the geometric counterpart of a recurrent algebraic operation, in this case of the successive doublings and triplings in the original numerical framework, and the octave-experience in particular calls for a circular representation. At the same time, of course, Plato is expressing the important theory that immortality is characterized by circular motion. The inner circle is divided into seven concentric parts, and these are in turn spaced according to the same double tetractys, so that the intervals between them are given by the series 1,2,3,4,8,9,27. They are then made to move at speeds which are various but which again are determined by proportional relationships. The soul of the world, as Plato tells us, partakes of reason and harmony.

Having made the soul, which is invisible, the Artificer constructs the sensible body of the cosmos. The visible planets and stars are placed in the circles of the other and the circle of the same respectively, and thus are arranged in the same mathematical-musical relationship as the soul itself. In the construction of the body the Artificer must deal with the realm of necessity, which fundamentally is the unformed extension in which the world is made. Impressed upon this extension but subservient to its inherent tendencies are the elementary geometric patterns of which the primary materials, the so-called elements, consist. These elements are originally fire and earth, but it is necessary to bind them together, and for this purpose geometric proportion is employed. This provides the most perfect bond, for the geometric mean fuses completely with the extremes.

Since the world is to be tridimensional, however, two means are required, and thus two additional elements, air and water, are placed between fire and earth in such a way that the four constitute a continuing geometric progression, the very series produced by the construction of Archytas. Thus the body of the world "was harmonized by proportion." But the elements must actually have some common substratum, for—with the exception of earth—they can be transmuted one into another. They are made up not of qualitative contraries but of geometric atoms too small to be seen.

Basically then, the sensible world consists not of gross matter but of mathematical structures imprinted upon space, a view which finds remarkable confirmation in twentieth-century science. Four of the Platonic solids—tetrahedrons, octahedrons, icosahedrons, and cubes—are the seeds of fire, air, water, and earth respectively, and different species of the elements are caused by seeds of different sizes. The ultimate atoms are really two types of triangles, the isosceles right triangle and the scalene right triangle that is half of an equilateral triangle, for these make up the faces of the regular solids. They also provide an explanation of transmutation, since the second type of triangle is a constituent common to fire, air, and water.

Although the simple construction of the regular solids used by Plato may have been his own discovery, it is more likely that it was developed by Theaetetus, or that it was known to the Pythagoreans, like most of the mathematics of the *Timaeus*. The constitution and properties of the elements also, then, are "perfected and harmonized in due proportion" by the Artificer. Finally in addition to the fundamental proportional relationship between the elements as a whole, particular proportions characterize their combination to make up the various objects of the world, both animate and inanimate. Thus all the compounds of the elements—the whole sensible world of becoming—are comparable to the material of the world soul, which is a proportioned mixture of components; and in their overall geometric layout as well, soul and body follow identical musical principles of order.

The mathematical instrument used to combine materials is the geometric mean; accordingly geometric progression is common to soul and body. But also, the particular aspect of the soul that corresponds to the perceptible courses of the heavenly bodies is appropriately patterned on a combination of two continuing geometric progressions of opposed nature, as given by the double tetractys. On the other hand, the detailed structure peculiar to the soul involves all three types of mean, an interesting counterpart of the fact that Archytas considered them all to belong to the domain of music. Yet the harmonic mean may very well have been regarded as the most fully adequate representation of harmony, and since harmony was typical of perfect structures, as specifically characteristic of the realm of purpose and the true knowledge of being. In any event, the mathematical construction of the soul comprises progressions of every type, all welded together in the unity of the musical scale.

The importance of the number 4 as a basis of harmonic order is seen once more in the tetrachord, the fundamental unit of the musical system and thus of the soul. And it is found also in the peopling of the world with four types of creatures constituted—apart from the matter of soul—of combinations of the four elements. The first are the immortal gods, who are the planets and stars themselves, and the other three are the mortal air, sea, and land animals. This provides a tetractys not mathematically defined, but correlated with the elements, each of which is peculiarly appropriate to one species of creature: fire, air, water, and earth are the predominant if not the sole constituents of the species of the heavens, air, water, and earth respectively. The Pythagoreans' worship of the tetractys may well have rested on the divinity of the elements along with that of number.

It becomes clear in the *Timaeus* that the generality of the conception of harmony in its application to the cosmos rests upon the unity of mathematics, and indeed this is the basis of its generality in every quantitative application, whether to world or man, or to society or art. But the unity of mathematics is in turn grounded in the nature of the world and of thought; the interconnection of the *mathemata* is by no means fortuitous.

From a psychological point of view the nocturnal sky may be the chief source of the Pythagorean mathematical outlook; it is a clear and impressive example of the identity of units and points, of number and geometric figure, of figure and physical object, even of mathematics and life. Taken together with the practice of representing number geometrically and physically, it almost compels the observation that number constitutes everything, and suggests pursuits such as that of Eurytus in seeking to determine the number of a horse or a man. Aristotle scoffed at such notions, including the idea that concepts such as justice might have numbers also, but scientific investigation eventually turned the whole physical world into number, and may very well do so with the biological and psychological worlds as well.

In any event, the unity of the mathematical disciplines is due in no small measure to the basic nature of the concept of harmony. Vibrating strings are an audible unity of number and length; ratio and proportion—the foundation of harmonics—play a vital part in arithmetic and geometry and astronomy; number itself arises from the harmony of opposites.

Plato deepens the theoretical basis of the interconnection of the branches of mathematics, partly by adding a powerful ethical constituent. But purely from a formal point of view, he appreciates fully the generality of harmony. Music is the final discipline because it is the most general and explains best the whole nature of mathematics; we might even say that as the study of relation it will logically deal with the relations between the various sciences. Its position as the last discipline also emphasizes its connection with motion as well as with relation; it becomes the counterpart of astronomy as audible rather than visible motion, or more general than astronomy as the motion of both number and figure. Plato makes it quite clear that music is of universal relevance: "Moreover, as I have now said several times, he who has not contemplated the mind of nature which is said to exist in the stars, and gone through the previous training, and seen the connection of music with these things, and harmonized them all with laws and institutions, is not able to give a reason of such things as have a reason." [23]

As far as the mathematical analysis of harmony is concerned, the importance of the *Timaeus* consists in making explicit a more advanced theory of the harmony of opposites and then generalizing it so that it applies also to more than two components. In this theoretical respect, the dialogue is actually an elaborate harmonic study, but because it contains as well an essentially universal treatment of the metaphysical, ethical, and aesthetic implications of harmony, its scope is still more remarkable. As we have seen, the *Symposium* advances the idea—which the *Philebus* later takes up in more explicit terms— that opposites require modification before they can be harmonized; some principle applied to both must make them compatible. (Their actual attraction can then be explained by the force of love.) But in the *Timaeus* the idea of binding the contraries with some third entity is made basic. The bond is mathematically conceived as a mean, and it is of the same nature as the elements to be harmonized. Thus the concept of opposites that are compatible and held together by an attractive force is replaced by the more abstract and general concept of a number of homogeneous elements standing in a determined relation to one another. But this notion of harmony gives rise to its own ethical qualities of love and goodness; it is also

applicable to more complex structures, such as the internal constitution of living beings; and it produces aesthetic values as well.

The cosmogony of the *Timaeus* is in essence a story of the creation of harmonic order, a concept that now includes ordered arrangement of a great many kinds; "when all things were in disor-
der, the Demiurge created in each thing in relation to itself, and in
all things in relation to each other, all the measures and harmonies
which they could possibly receive." [24] But in addition, it becomes
obvious that the harmonic view of the world is not purely an objective picture of structure. Value is apparently an inevitable feature of
cosmology, as it is of myth and to some extent of natural science as
well. Divine embodiments of natural forces are the rule in theogony,
and the same procedure even enhances the value of ethical forces. In
philosophical thought, Eros is gradually transformed into the cosmic
force of love, which manifests itself in the harmony of opposites.
Harmony itself, once a goddess born of divine opposites, remains a
concept charged with value; and this is part of the reason that it
increasingly replaces more colorless descriptions of combination,
such as equilibrium, balance, and mixture, and even comes to control the temporal concepts of measure and rhythm, as it does in the
Timaeus. Paired principles, again descended from gods, are no less
infused with value. The divinities of Heaven and Earth become the
forces of light and dark, and distant descendants like sameness and
otherness still contain transformed concepts of good and bad. Even
the apparently distinct conception of mind bears a relation to the
traditional contraries, for it is opposed to matter somewhat as fire is
to night, as good is to bad. But like love, which is paired with the
evil of strife, mind becomes an ordering force separate from paired
elements, concealing its history in its positive character. In any
event, the incorporation into the world of a rational principle of
order means the attribution to nature of purpose and also of beauty
in a deeper sense than unreasoned symmetry.

Wherever we look the role of value in cosmology is confirmed. If it is mind in the case of Anaxagoras, it is justice in Anaximander, love in Empedocles, and harmony itself in Heraclitus. To the Pythagoreans in much greater degree than to other philosophers, with the possible exception of Plato, the order of the cosmos was ethical and religious as well as physical and metaphysical. Number itself was bound up with value, for it was either the essential or the sole constituent of everything, apparently even of justice; the "holy tetractys" is simply the most prominent example of a general outlook. Perhaps more important still was the faith with which the Pythagoreans pursued the traces of number in the world; their search for harmony was part of a belief, and their science an expression of mysticism. There are remnants and counterparts of this attitude in the religious faith with which many scientists regard the mathematical order of the world in modern times, and in human dedication to science; the search for truth, although dispassionate in one sense, can become a way of life, and research a moral value.

Under the influence of the predominantly ethical outlook of Socrates, considerations of the good affected every department of Plato's thought, and the outspoken teleology of his world endows its order with profound value. Cosmic harmony is the direct expression of the Artificer's desire that the world be good. The place made for the cosmic soul is especially important, for in its very conception the soul is both good and beautiful, and it embodies these values in its harmony. Goodness characterizes not only the soul, however, but the whole cosmos; the Artificer wanted everything to be as like himself as possible, an end which he achieves through harmonious order in every part of his work. Even if the cosmogony of the *Timaeus*—unlike those of myth and religion—is actually an allegory that expounds a cosmology by the fictional device of narration, the good in the cosmos is one of the properties that Plato earnestly seeks to explain. The ordered and ordering intelligence of the world soul will still be both good and a force for good, and this value will inform the material sphere also. But if the teleological conception of the cosmos is the most prominent basis for the value that inheres in its harmony, the conception of the cosmos as alive is important too, for only an organism can fully incorporate purpose and goodness. The cosmic soul, like the Artificer himself, is a transposition of an anthropological discovery; it carries over into the universe the consciousness of the human power of artistic creation. In terms of the cosmogonic narrative, only a cosmos that is alive can be made close in goodness to the Artificer.

The theory of classes and their interrelationship that Plato expounds variously in the *Sophist* and the *Philebus* contains a conception of harmony that is more or less distinct from cosmogony and possesses an even greater generality than the harmonic ideas of the *Timaeus*. The kind of theory involved is an outcome of the critique developed in the *Parmenides,* which exposed defects in the conception of the Platonic Ideas and also in the Eleatic doctrine of being that is fundamental to the Ideas. The denial of reality to anything but a monolithic Being that admits no opposite or difference also obstructs a positive result in the epistemological investigation of the *Theaetetus:* the definition of knowledge appears to demand the existence of non-being and of falsehood. The difficulties reappear in the *Sophist,* where a solution is found in the notion of the mingling or communion of classes of existence. Instead of emphasizing the transcendental aspect of these concepts of class, as he does in presenting the theory of Ideas in the *Timaeus,* Plato treats them simply as genera or categories, for his concern is with logical method in its own right rather than with metaphysics. The possible relationships between genera are defined: a given class may communicate or intermix with no other, with some others, or with all others. In particular, Plato selects five of the principal categories—being, rest, motion, the same, the other—and investigates their communion with one another. This undertaking is the proper subject of the art or science of dialectic. Music, or harmonics, is the science of knowing what mingles and what does not in connection with sound, and philosophy pursues the same kind of science with respect to classes.

The harmonic nature of dialectical inquiry becomes much more conspicuous in the related discussion of classes in the *Philebus*. Plato does not select genera from those of importance, but instead undertakes to apply division to the whole of existence, and arrives at four classes: the infinite, the finite, the compound, and the cause. The class of the finite (or the definite or limited) includes the equal and the double, and any other ratio of number and measure; it is consequently able to end difference and opposition, and to create harmony and proportion among different elements by the introduction of number. As a result, the compound or mixed class, which is the union or offspring of the first two, is essentially the category of the harmonious. The generation of this class is brought about by the fourth one, that of cause. The whole system is nothing more or less than a scheme of the generation of harmony, and it makes harmony the central characteristic of existence as well as of philosophy. Behind the classes of the infinite and the finite we can discern the Pythagorean hypostases of the unlimited dyad and the monad which enter into the harmonic generation of number.

In keeping with the notion advanced in the *Symposium* that opposed elements must be modified before they can be harmonized, the account in the *Philebus* does not combine opposed elements, but mingles the various opposites of the infinite class with factors of the finite class to produce certain forms of harmonic nature. When heat and cold prevail, for example, the introduction of the principles of the limited takes away excess and indefiniteness, and infuses moderation and harmony. But of greater importance than the seasons, or than health and strength, are the ethical examples of harmony, for the *Philebus* is concerned primarily with determing the good, and the harmonic conceptions are completely general. Socrates, whose exceptional appearance as an important protagonist of a late dialogue is undoubtedly due to the subject matter of the discussion, is particularly concerned with the applications to ethics: "O my beautiful Philebus, the goddess, methinks, seeing the universal wantonness and wickedness of all things, and that there was in them no limit to pleasures and self-indulgence, devised the limit of law and order." [25] To the mixed or harmonious class belongs the mixed life of pleasure and wisdom, acknowledged as the best; and this class also contains the origin of bodily pleasures and pains, for living beings are made up of the natural union of the finite and infinite. They are, in a word, harmonic structures.

When the harmony in animals is dissolved there is also a dissolution of nature and a generation of pain, while the restoration of harmony and return to nature is the source of pleasure. An analysis of the different kinds of pleasure and wisdom permits a more detailed determination of the constitution of the mixed life; and with the results of such an analysis as materials, Socrates mixes together the components of this best life after the fashion of artistic creation. The finished work would appear to be characterized most importantly by harmony, for the most precious element of the mixture and therefore the highest good of all is found in the appropriate proportions of the constituents. Without measure and the mean and the suitable, the mixture would not be a mixture, but only a confused medley. The second highest good also, which consists in the class of the symmetrical, the beautiful, and the perfect, has something of a harmonic nature; what is more, symmetry possesses aesthetic as well as ethical value, if we can characterize as aesthetic the highly abstract beauty of a category of the good. There can be no doubt, however, that the role in which Plato has cast Socrates is very close to that of a musical composer. The answer to hedonism in ethics is not the denial of pleasure, but the application of harmony.

The Greek philosophy of man is long in developing principles and concepts peculiar to the human sphere; it borrows heavily from cosmology and natural philosophy, and as a result, the conceptions of harmony found in anthropology are often not original to the field. In their new setting, however, the borrowed ideas take on a new significance, and this in turn can affect cosmological thought. Anthropological ideas develop chiefly in the field of medical theory, with appears first in close association with Pythagoreanism. Alcmaeon of Croton,[26] a physician of southern Italy who was active in the early fifth century B.C., described health as a balance and a proportionate mixture of qualities in the body; the commensurability of the paired opposites in the mixture was based on the simple relation of equality. On the other hand, he conceived the soul as continually in motion; it was immortal because it was similar to the immortal heavens. But could this motion of the soul have been circular? Alcmaeon seems to imply that it is in holding that man dies because he is unable to join the beginning to the end. Accordingly, this philosopher may have influenced the Pythagorean theory of both body and soul, for Simmias' concept of the harmony of the body in the *Phaedo* could very well have been derived from the simpler notion of health as *isonomia,* just as the description of the soul in the *Timaeus* could easily go back to an earlier concept of circular motion. At the same time, neither bodily *isonomia* or harmony nor circular motion in the soul can be discovered in Pythagorean thought before Alcmaeon.

In the physical realm, of course, any general theory of harmony will apply equally to man and nature. In Empedocles' view, for example, man too is a harmony of the four elements caused by love.[27] Temporal and social and qualitative concepts of harmony are suggested also: love is responsible for harmonious actions and friendly thoughts.[28] In the Hippocratic writings,[29] health is discussed as a balance of the four qualities—cold, hot, wet, dry—which, like the Empedoclean elements, are also found in nature, specifically in the seasons. Hippocratic medicine typically viewed health against the background of physical environment, and regarded climate as the determinant of bodily constitution. This was actually a cosmic connection, since antiquity knows no distinction in principle between meteorology and astronomy. Thus the cyclic predominance of the qualities in man follows their succession in the seasons, and the correspondence between world and man is deepened into a causal connection. Similarly in the *Nature of Man,* health is described as an equilibrium of four humors—black bile, yellow bile, blood, and phlegm—and in each season a different humor predominates. In later times, these theories were complemented by Galen's somewhat different conception of the four temperaments, each of which was a blend of qualities and elements and humors; the elaboration of classical ideas was characteristic of late antiquity.

Temporal concepts of harmony are more at home in the human than in the natural province; the Hippocratic writings often bring rhythm under the head of harmony. There are examples in the progress of fevers, which revealed distinctive numerical patterns in the recurrence of critical days, thus permitting confirmation of the symptoms of the disease and making prognosis possible. Such patterns were specifically conceived as ordered numerical progressions of a harmonic nature. Health, too, was brought within the sphere of temporal harmony, for it was signified to the physician when he judged the rhythms of the pulse and of breathing to be harmonious. Most striking of all is the Pythagorean element that enters the discussion of embryology.[30] The growth of the embryo followed a harmonic pattern of days; particular stages of development were reached in specified times. The embryo was viewed as a musical instrument, and embryonic development became a musical performance.

The concept of the harmony of the body, as it developed in the Pythagorean-Empedoclean-Hippocratic tradition of philosophic medicine, receives its most systematic exposition in the speech of Eryximachus in Plato's *Symposium.*[31] Since the *Symposium* deals with various types of love and their relative values, Plato's physician advances the notion of two kinds of love, only one of which knows moderation and thus leads to harmony, while the other (which is clearly Empedoclean strife in disguise) is evil and leads to excess.

But the important point here is the generality of this ethical basis of harmonic structure; although love is a specifically human concept in origin, it becomes the foundation for harmony of every type. The theoretical analysis of harmony also, which we have discussed above, applies with equal force both to the harmony of nature and the harmony of man. If we add to these factors the causal role of the seasons and the weather and the harmonic conception of rhythm, the full breadth of the medical theory of harmony becomes apparent. The generalization of this theory—which reaches here and there into astronomical, religious, social, and qualitative concepts of harmony—is the main achievement of the discourse.

An important theory of the harmony of the soul is advanced in Plato's *Phaedo* [32] by the Theban Simmias, who is a disciple of Philolaus. He maintains that the soul is a harmony of the body and illustrates his meaning by comparing the body to a lyre. Although the idea is materialistic, it is not completely unable to account for certain cherished properties of the soul; even though Simmias makes harmony dependent upon physical materials, he recognizes its incorporeal and divine nature. The conception is thoroughly Pythagorean as far as number and harmony are concerned, but it is quite the contrary in its insistence on the soul's mortality, curiously contradicting the Pythagorean belief in metempsychosis. The physical world becomes a basis of explanation in a realm long since recognized as fundamentally different, and that is why Socrates (the man chiefly responsible for formulating the Western concept of the soul) advances a series of detailed refutations.[33] These cannot be taken to imply, of course, that he opposes the notion that the soul is harmonic or harmonious in nature; he takes issue only with the particular idea that the body furnishes the elements of such a harmony. The soul exists before birth, he maintains, adducing the recollection of the Ideas as evidence, but a harmony cannot exist before the elements that compose it come into being. The soul may be evil or contain vice, but a harmony cannot be inharmonious or contain discord. Again the soul controls and leads the body, while a harmony cannot influence its elements but in fact depends upon them. Thus Socrates defeats an argument that would demonstrate the mortality of the soul, for just as the harmony of the lyre vanishes upon destruction of the instrument, so the soul would perish upon the death of the body.

On the other hand, Plato conceives the soul not as identical with harmony but as containing harmony, and not as dependent upon physical elements but as composed of its own specific material. In the *Republic* the soul is described as tripartite;[34] it consists of rational, spirited, and appetitive principles. Temperance is a harmony between these three parts, a condition in which the rational principle exercises control over the other two. Discord is equivalent to evil. The structural aspect of the conception becomes still clearer in the comparison between the principles and the strings of a musical instrument.[35] Aside from this harmony, however, Plato also gives his attention to the relation between the rational and spirited parts only,[36] leaving the appetitive part out of the consideration. Ostensibly he is then concerned with a different kind of harmony, that between soul and body, which is effected by the action of music on the one and gymnastics on the other; but he actually regards the body only as a tool by means of which gymnastics affects the spirited principle of the soul, while music acts on its rational or philosophical principle. Thus the spirited part of the soul is brought into harmony with the rational part; it is adjusted—like the string of a musical instrument, Plato says—through gymnastics.

A much more elaborate picture of the harmony of the soul is found in the *Timaeus*.[37] Like the world soul, the human soul is blended of sameness, otherness, and intermediate existence, which is itself a compound of indivisible existence and divisible existence; but in man these constituents are somewhat diluted. Again as he did in the case of the cosmic soul, the Artificer divides the compounded material into a series of quantities arranged in order and size accord-

ing to the double tetractys and the Dorian diatonic scale, and sets up
the group of revolving circles spaced according to the same tetractys.
This operation does not complete the construction of the human
soul, however, as it does that of its cosmic counterpart, but yields
only its rational or divine part; the work is then given over to the
created gods (who in general are the artisans of the realm of necessity) so that they may complete it by constructing the mortal parts
of the soul—its emotional and appetitive parts—from a harmony of the
four sensible elements. The three sections of the soul, housed appropriately in the head, thorax, and abdomen, form an additional harmony among themselves, which, as in the *Republic,* is characterized
by the control of reason over emotion and appetite. Dominance of
one of the constituents of the harmony is found in the rational part
of the soul also, where the circle of the same, the outermost one, is
given dominance over the circles of the other.

Attention need hardly be called to the role of value in human
harmony. While nature is generally equated to the physical world
and even thought of as inanimate, man is conceived of at least
as early as the fifth century B.C. as a combination of the two vastly
different entities of body and soul, and the large place of ethical
values is consequently insured. The ordered state of the body means
physical health; the ordered state of the soul means mental and
emotional health and also reason. Thus harmony is more obviously
a good in man than in the cosmos, where its full value hinges upon
our acceptance of a teleological and organic view of nature.

The ethical value of human harmony takes its most prominent
form in the harmony of virtue, which is discussed frequently by
Plato. To the extent that virtues are considered as residing in the
soul, they are part of the conception of the harmony of man; but
such a conception is very readily transferred to society and to the
world, and in its extreme form becomes the abstract ethical harmony of the *Philebus.* Another tendency of the harmony of virtue is
that it easily loses its structural and quantitative character and turns

into a generalized equilibrium and quieting of conflicting desires and feelings in the soul and finally into a purely qualitative "harmony of life" associated typically with a feeling of joy or happiness. Harmony is called joy as early as Empedocles, although in his case the explanation lies in the basic role of love. And in the fragmentary writings of Democritus, both social harmony and also the joy that results from a harmonious life appear in a completely figurative light, since they are unaccompanied by any cosmological or mathematical conceptions of harmony. Ideas of harmony often emphasize pleasure and neglect structure. The underlying conception can be that of a mean value itself as a harmony; thus a harmonious voice is one that has a well-chosen intermediate nature in respect of pitch and loudness, although it can also be one that is simply pleasant in quality. In such qualitative conceptions of harmony, which proliferate endlessly, there are generally some vague implications either of mean values or of compatible constituents, but the mathematical structure is really of no importance and cannot be specified. Yet Plato often harmonizes and weaves virtues in a quite specific sense; the harmony of the virtues in the *Republic* has a literal meaning, and justice and temperance consist in fact of harmonized components.[38] The consideration of virtue even uncovers the theoretic fact— so wonderfully illustrated in musical concord—that the components of a harmony (in this case justice) must preserve their individuality in spite of their relationship; harmony is not fusion.[39] In the soul itself, the harmony of the principles is a close parallel to the harmony of qualities, elements, or humors in the physical world.

Society can be thought of as occupying a middle ground between man and the world of nature. Modes of thought and conceptual models flow back and forth among all three fields, and ideas of harmony are inevitably imported into the social sphere from both the others. If the connection between society and the natural world appears to be especially influential in early Greek thought, the relationship between society and man becomes more important in classical times. A conspicuous concept deriving from the legal sphere and entering cosmology is that of justice and retribution; but conversely, Solon's concepts of justice were formulated partly as a parallel to his notions of law in nature. But as far as harmony is concerned, social concepts are derived mostly from anthropology.

Plato regards society and the individual as parallel; in general, if harmony characterizes the relationships within man, it equally characterizes those between men. Lovers pass their lives in harmony,[40] but the bad, because they are at variance and enmity with themselves, are not in union or harmony with one another.[41] The harmony of society is especially important in the *Republic,* where it occurs in a variety of forms.

There are four classes of society: gold, silver, bronze, and iron; and in these are to be found the larger social counterparts of the principles contained in the individual human soul. Indeed the whole motivation of the dialogue depends upon this parallel, for virtue is to be examined as it occurs in the state, in the hope of better comprehending it in its more conspicuous form. Plato projects a detailed correspondence between individual and state. In both spheres, harmony is defined in much the same terms; the musical scale provides the formal basis, with its connection between high, low, and middle tones, and its fitting together of all the intermediate degrees. This type of relationship characterizes the natural order of the principles in man, and it has a particular illustration in the order of the three parts of the soul. Temperance in the individual is a harmonious relationship; justice in human nature, both in body and soul, means that the elements within man cooperate and do not mutually interfere. And in society also, temperance "runs through all the notes of the scale, and produces a harmony of the weaker and stronger and the middle class, whether you suppose them to be stronger or weaker in wisdom or power or number or wealth, or anything else."[42] Like musical tones, which have their specific identities and functions in music, each element of man or of the state does its own work, not interfering or coalescing with the others, but cooperating to form the harmony of temperance and justice.

Throughout the dialogue the conceptions of harmony are so numerous and so important that they actually govern the argument and provide a basis for its organization and aesthetic form. Even mathematical details, such as the law according to which human births are best regulated, are often in some degree harmonic in nature; but most symptomatic of all, the central concept of justice, traditionally conceived as a temporal balance and compensation, turns out upon investigation to be a form of harmony. Thus the *Republic* arrives at a view of society that is parallel to the view of macrocosm and microcosm achieved later in the *Timaeus*.

Accordingly it is possible for conceptions of harmony to facilitate the transfer of concepts between these fields, giving structure and substance to borrowed models of thought and making them more precisely suited to their explanatory purpose. But the correspondences between man and society and nature, and those between body and soul also, come to be regarded as additional types of harmony, such as the harmony between society and cosmos, or between man and cosmos, or between body and soul. If we take into account as well the harmonic conceptions of the arts, the world of experience assumes a remarkable symmetry, the detailed form of which is due to the almost numberless ramifications of harmonic ideas. Both the multitude of meanings and the extent to which they correspond are surprising. The musician creates harmony in the pitch and duration of tone and in gesture; man creates harmony in the conduct of his life; the statesman creates harmony in society; the Demiurge creates harmony in the cosmos; the philosopher creates the harmony of dialectic and the music of discourse.

These are all artists or scientists—there is no distinction between the two—proceeding on the basis of knowledge and imposing order on their materials. Since their purpose is clear, they need not either rely on inspiration or imitate mere appearance. Instead they have probable opinion, based on experience, of the nature and properties of their materials, and true knowledge, based on reason, of the models to which they work.

Many of Plato's conceptions of harmony can conveniently be brought under the head of the general notion that philosophy itself is harmonic or musical. A simple instance is that harmony can become a criterion of consistency in reasoning, as this is manifested in the agreement of ideas. "Certainly there should be harmony," says Socrates humorously in the *Phaedo,* "in a discourse whose subject is harmony." [43] And in the *Gorgias* this conception is combined with the idea that discourse or dialectic in general is music; [44] Socrates warns Callicles that if he does not refute the thesis that has been advanced he will never be at one with himself, and his whole life will be a discord, while Socrates, on the other hand, would rather that his lyre be inharmonious and that there be no music in the chorus he provides, or that the whole world should be at odds with him and oppose him, than that he should be at odds with himself and contradict himself. The abstract nature of the conception of harmony is revealed here in the lower value placed on the musical as opposed to the logical variety.

This is also a feature of the reference to harmony in the *Laches*:[45] the true musician is attuned to a fairer harmony than that of the lyre, for he has arranged in his life a harmony of words and deeds which is in the Dorian mode, the true Hellenic one. The concept so ingeniously developed here is really a variant of the notion of consistency in argument. As these examples show, the agreement of ideas, or of words and deeds, can also become a harmony in human life, thus furnishing a parallel—although it lacks the suggestion of mathematical structure—to the harmony of the parts of the soul, which is equated in the *Republic* to a harmonious life.[46] The philosopher in particular is thought of as having a harmonious nature.

Actually the whole method of division in discourse, of the determination of genera and species, which Plato comes to regard as central to dialectic, is also a harmonic process; as we have seen, the application of the method in the *Philebus* is probably the most all-embracing and abstract example of harmony in the whole of Plato's writings. Preceding this harmonic division of existence there is a methodological discussion that makes use of music as a remarkably appropriate illustration,[47] and thus serves to confirm the inherently harmonic nature of philosophic method.

With the conception of philosophy as an example of harmony, or, more typically, as the highest music, a circle closes in the history of Greek harmonic ideas, and the abstract meaning of harmony, which music so importantly determined, leads back to the concept of actual sonority; for philosophy can be thought of as music almost as much in a literal as in a figurative sense. The study of harmonics crystallizes the conception of harmony in its abstract significance; Socrates complains insistently in the *Republic* about those who limit the discipline to relationships that are audible, and he characterizes the subject as fundamentally different from the study of music.[48] But harmonics, which scorns sonority, leads to the ultimate goal of education, the "hymn of dialectic."

That this peculiarly equivocal conception of harmony and music had a central position in Plato's thought is suggested by the number of times it occurs in his writings and by the large variety of forms it takes. Socrates is an aulos player whose art of dialectic is a peculiarly persuasive music; a potential victim must stop up his ears as he would to the song of the Sirens.[49] The last essay of Socrates in the art of dialectic is his swan song.[50] He at first could not understand the injunction he often received in his dreams to compose music, for he had always practiced philosophy, and this was certainly the highest and best music.[51] Similarly, in the myth of the grasshoppers that Socrates narrates in the *Phaedrus*,[52] Calliope and Urania are the Muses concerned with philosophers and their music, with heaven and thought, and they themselves have the sweetest utterance. Invocations to the Muses are in fact common in the dialogues, and Plato undoubtedly regarded his works as a superior kind of poetry. That these conceptions of the musical nature of philosophy have a literal meaning is indicated by their concern with musical effects upon man, for it is primarily in acoustic qualities and the significance of sung words that the influences of music reside.

In the writings of Plato, Greek conceptions of harmony achieve their maximum diffusion and influence, leaving no major sphere of philosophy unaffected, and in a sense fulfilling Heraclitus' thesis of the universality of the harmonic logos. This universality is no longer a characteristic of the outlook of Aristotle and the Peripatetic philosophers; harmony remains a versatile conceptual tool, but various factors—an increased empiricism, the denial of the transcendental nature of numbers and the Ideas, a more objective comprehension of philosophic problems—conspire to contract its meaning and to restrict it to a particular kind of mathematical pattern useful in analysis. Yet the Platonic diversity was never really lost and in spite of transformations and curtailment has persisted or recurred as a permanent heritage of Western thought.

II. Theories of Musical Ethics

Concepts of the ethical force of music are a characteristic feature of the Greek outlook; long before they become explicit in philosophy they are expressed both in myths of musical magic and in various fields of musical practice, which involve more properly ethical if less spectacular effects. Myth, religion, medicine, and ceremony all unite to give moral concepts their strength and diversity, and these formulations do not simply disappear with the advent of philosophic thought; their contribution to ethical theory is especially significant because they continue on alongside philosophy, giving it depth and social relevance.

Myths that tell of the power of music are concerned primarily with the compulsive character of human response; thus it is not surprising to find man in the company of animals, plants, and inanimate nature. The irresistible and fatal attraction of the Sirens has its parallel in the fascination Arion exercised over dolphins, or in Amphion's ability to make stones arrange themselves in order, while the universal influence exerted by Orpheus extends from nature to the gods. It is accordingly the suspension of the will that appears as the most striking feature of musical magic; the action of music is so direct and potent that it knows no resistance. Most typically a kind of hypnosis is produced, an enchantment in which the hearer is rendered motionless; yet we can say that the music affects feeling as well as will, for the influence is a total one in which the faculties are not distinguished.

The mental cures of orgiastic ritual are quite different. We are still in the magical province of physical medicine when Odysseus' wound is stanched by a chant,[1] but in Dionysiac rites we leave magic for matters of fact.[2] Both the Thracian cult of Bacchus and the related Phrygian cult of Cybele made use of wild dance and music, with the effect of purgation and purification. The fervent and stimulating character of the music was due to a great extent to the aulos, an instrument also played with intoxicating effect by Marsyas, the Phrygian nature god who is the counterpart of Pan. In Plato's *Laws*,[3] dance and the syrinx are made responsible for quieting the frenzy of the Bacchantes, while in the *Ion*,[4] we learn that during the dancing of the Corybantian mysteries the revelers were not in their right minds. Orgiastic practices are connected in general with Asiatic religion, with Thrace and Phrygia, and they form a sharp contrast to the more characteristically Greek myths of musical magic, which revolve around the use of the lyre and the voice, and are centered in calm rather than excitement. Again, however, feeling is not distinct from will; there is a highly emotional but also thoroughly compulsive response. But in addition, the essentially magical effects of tone and of particular melodies are joined by a direct and frenzied participation; to the stimulus of melody there is added the excitement of dance, and finally the purging and purification that are the more indirect but equally intrinsic effect of the whole.

Thus music is both a cure and a cause of the agitation, for if it does not produce the disturbance altogether, it certainly brings about an intensification.[5] The resultant cure, accordingly, is homeopathic rather than allopathic; the final calm—or exhaustion—is not the outcome of soothing music but of catharsis or emotional discharge. These rites are evidently quite like the epileptic fits of the shaman, the dancing epidemics of the Middle Ages, the seventeenth-century outbreaks of tarantism, or the uncontrollable jerking of American revivalist meetings; probably in every case, religion is an essential factor.

Thus we are dealing not only with a medical phenomenon but also with a spiritual one, not simply with a purification but with a heightening of human power until it becomes identified with divinity. In terms of religious procedures, this is the route of mysticism rather than reason, or of emotion rather than contemplation; it is turned inward to the divine in man rather than outward to the heavens. Indeed the myth of the devouring of Dionysus by the Titans made it possible to account for the presence of god in man, and the mystic experiences fostered by intoxication and music provided a confirmation. In a transient type of madness the soul was ecstatically separated from the body; its divine nature enabled it to achieve mantic power. But most important of all is the fact that rite involves an element of imitation, which readily enters along with dance. The imitation takes the form of pantomime, but not as a conscious art exercised with detachment; instead it becomes an identification of the initiates with the actual followers of Dionysus, and through them, with the god himself. In this activity we have the archetype of mimesis and of drama; imitation—like Greek educational and ethical concepts in general—is associated originally with music and pantomimic dance rather than with painting and sculpture. And it is the imitative aspect of religious orgy that makes it comparable to normal educational procedures as well as entailing a greater concreteness in the nature of music.

The Orphic movement of the sixth century B.C., by contrast, reveals conceptions close to those of musical myth. Although Orphism continues to pay allegiance to Dionysus, it actually represents the fruitful composite of the Dionysian and Apollonian cults which was manifested most conspicuously in the Delphic shrine. Clear perception and knowledge—the whole visual mentality eventually consummated in the Platonic Ideas—become important factors, along with the instrument of Apollo, the lyre. The religious amalgamation can almost be thought of as a new influence of music on the Apollonian outlook. With it all, Orphism remained mystical; its aim was to purify the soul; its prophet, although often considered to be the son of Apollo, was a Thracian musical magician.

Elaborate doctrine was added to rite, and mythical thought moved closer to philosophy. The dual nature of man and the immortality of the soul were clearly formulated in the concept of transmigration, and the primitive Dionysian cult, which had developed centuries earlier, was elaborated into a whole monastic code of life. With Dionysus become an Olympian god, only remnants of the original chthonian aspect of orgiastic ritual were preserved in the wheel of birth and its interesting parallel of Orpheus' trip to the underworld. But in general the Dionysian heritage is easily seen; Herodotus mentions the "rites called Orphic and Bacchic" in one breath,[6] and Orpheus himself is torn apart by the maenads quite like the sacrificial bull of the Bacchic communion, although his fate might have been earned by apostasy.

We cannot doubt that the concept of music had been radically changed; the Orphics are concerned with the lyre and the voice rather than the aulos, with enchantment rather than frenzy, and even prophecy takes on a reasonable instead of a rapturous character. Dance is apparently absent, while the appearance of song means that some contribution is made by the specifically rational element of music. In general, music is no longer an inarticulate outpouring of emotion given form only by pantomime, but a harmonic science with a tonal as well as a verbal logos. This is all a concomitant of an interest in the purification of the soul rather than its identification with divinity, and of a reliance on asceticism and freedom from contamination rather than exhilaration and frenzy.

The most important of the Orphic sects were the Pythagoreans, and they seem to have added an Egyptian element to the movement; Herodotus goes so far as to state that the Orphic rites were really Egyptian and Pythagorean.[7] Possibly it was this constituent that transformed Orphism, moving it in the direction of philosophy and science, which were capable of new growth and wider influence. Eventually there was a division between the esoteric, or religious, Pythagoreans, who were known as *akousmatikoi,* and the exoteric, or scientific, group, known as *mathematikoi.* The two parties differed not only with respect to their interests, but also because the one was monastic and the other public in its way of life.

The novel characteristics of Pythagorean thought are evident in the change they effected in cosmogony. The Orphic cosmogony extends the Hesiodic by its tendency to personify abstractions; it is still a theogony, but its gods are often concepts expressed in an old form. In the Pythagorean cosmogony, which we have discussed in the preceding chapter, there is still a formal correspondence with the Orphic hierarchical picture of divinities, but the gods themselves have disappeared, leaving only traces behind in the creative monad and the indefinite dyad. Mythology has with this step become philosophy; and although the mathematical studies of the brotherhood, as we have seen, reflect in their very constitution the dominant position of music, there can be no doubt that a new and higher purification was discovered, and that theory was substituted for sonority. Even the stress on abstinence and asceticism in the conduct of life has unmistakable implications for the kind of music the Pythagoreans may have employed, if indeed they employed any at all; for Neo-Py-thagorean legends notwithstanding, it is quite possible that the Pythagoreans turned away more or less completely from sensory experience, even from that which might involve tenuous emotions, and towards quiet contemplation and speculative thought. Certainly the later "so-called Pythagoreans" to whom Aristotle refers [8] were mathematicians; the *akousmatikoi* disappeared with little trace, and we can only conjecture about the nature of their practices, although the religious society, still more than the private philosophic or poetic school, is not unlikely to have made some use of music, perhaps in a fashion close to that of the medieval cloister.

In any event, it is the soothing effect of music that will bear a direct relation to knowledge and harmony; even the Sirens, who would appear to represent the purely sonorous magic of tone, promise knowledge to Odysseus and attract him partly for this reason also.[9] Words can be combined with the lyre but not with the aulos, and Aristotle is not indulging in a casual fancy when he interprets Athena's rejection of the aulos as an expression of her attribute of knowledge, and of the fact that the instrument contributes nothing to the mind.[10]

Plato takes the orgiastic effects of music very seriously indeed and tries to explain them and generalize them so that they are applicable to normal educational procedures. He even comes to classify education in general as a type of purification.[11] Just as he retains myth in his dialogues for those purposes that are outside the province of dialectic, so he is really not willing in his ethics to abandon either the orgiastic or the hypnotic effects of music. Even philosophic discourse, itself a kind of music, takes on a magical aspect, and Socrates is described as casting a spell over Meno, and enchanting him.[12] Plato may reject the aulos in the *Republic*,[13] but this severity—necessitated by a higher cause—can become admiration elsewhere. When Alcibiades compares Socrates to Marsyas, for example, all the powers of music over the human soul appear as achievements which philosophy emulates:

And are you not an aulos player? That you are, and a performer far more wonderful than Marsyas. He indeed with instruments used to charm the souls of man by the powers of his breath, and the players of his music do so still: for the melodies of Olympus are derived from Marsyas who taught them, and these, whether they are played by a great master or by a miserable aulos-girl, have a power which no others have; they alone possess the soul and reveal the wants of those who have need of gods and mysteries, because they are divine. But you produce the same effect with your words only, and do not require the aulos; that is the difference between you and him. When we hear any other speaker, even a very good one, he produces absolutely no effect upon us, or not much, whereas the mere fragments of you and your words, even at second-hand, and however imperfectly repeated, amaze and possess the souls of every man, woman, and child who comes within hearing of them. And if I were not afraid that you would think me hopelessly drunk, I would have sworn as well as spoken to the influence which they have always had and still have over me. For my heart leaps within me more than that of any Corybantian reveler, and my eyes rain tears when I hear them. And I observe that many others are affected in the same manner. I have heard Pericles and other great orators, and I thought that they spoke well, but I never had any similar feeling; my soul was not stirred by them, nor was I angry at the thought of my own slavish state. But this Marsyas has often brought me to such a pass, that I have felt as if I could hardly endure the life which I am leading (this, Socrates, you will admit); and I am conscious that if I did not shut my ears against him, and fly as from the voice of the Siren, my fate would be like that of others,—he would transfix me, and I should grow old sitting at his feet. For he makes me confess that I ought not to live as I do, neglecting the wants of my own soul, and busying myself with the concerns of the Athenians; therefore I hold my ears and tear myself away from him.[14]

Here we have a depiction both of the emotional potency of music and of the compound of seductiveness and knowledge. The passage is remarkable in the care with which it elaborates the details of its comparison; the madness of Alcibiades even contains a counterpart of the alcoholic stimulation that was combined with the music of the Dionysian rites.

The chief basis of the ethical philosophy of music, however, is not magic and orgy, but the customary educational and social uses of the art. There is obviously an interrelationship between these fields of musical practice; the ethical value of music cannot be confined to formal education, for schooling simply foreshadows, or more usually echoes, life in general: the place of music in education should provide a view of its place in society, or in society as it once was or desires itself to be. And at the same time, social occasions not explicitly defined as educative may be of the greatest significance in molding ideals and character.

Even though they can be distinguished readily from magical and orgiastic effects, the values of musical practice have some basis in religion and rite, for music is invariably the main constituent of commemorative ritual. Celebrations of heroes or of important historical events are intrinsically educative ceremonies. Participants come to know the ideals of society as these are manifested in deeds and in men; they learn to admire and to emulate particular virtues and moral characters. The whole process takes place by means of music; cultural values are embodied in words, dance, and melody, becoming the basis of specific musical genres—of closely defined styles and types of melody with particular ethical natures. And ritually significant music of this kind has divine sanction as well; the commemorated event has the approval of the gods, one of whom, especially involved, may even supply the melody or the appropriate instrument. Divinely originated, music must then be preserved and refashioned by successive composer-performers who take up each defined occasion of use. Even to the auditors, the strength of the effect is far above that of absolute music; it is not possible to comprehend such an ethical world from the vantage point of pure art. In the characteristic Greek setting, music is given the utmost force by social tradition and religious belief, and the concreteness it assumes is due ultimately to its real context of community ideals as concentrated in the decisive historic event that in part brought them about and at the same time exemplified them most fully for the edification of future generations. The music in question here is actually a representational art of rhythm: music-poetry-dance. Hellenic theories of musical ethics are generally concerned with music in this fuller form.

The component arts were on occasion separated, of course, although much less often and much less completely than we might think. If unaccompanied dance existed at all, it was not of much importance, while pure instrumental music was not only relatively unimportant, but also either explicitly programmatic or doubtless in its form, melody, and rhythm especially full of meaning derived from visual and verbal and kinesthetic experience. On the other hand, singing and speaking are very close in all ancient civilizations, very much as they are in primitive cultures; the two verbs themselves are coupled or used interchangeably, and in numberless literary descriptions we cannot tell whether speech or song is in question.

This ambiguity has a counterpart in the indeterminate nature of much preserved Greek poetry, for which melody, like dance, was unrecorded, although the euphony of the language, the qualities of the feeling expressed, and especially the meter, will often point unequivocally either to speaking or to singing. The complex relationships of duration can be such as to make spoken performance out of the question unless we are to omit completely the rhythmical features of the music (along with the melodic ones); the durations can be measured only by means of the precise power of temporal judgment that we can secure through tone. In its original forms, poetry was invariably musical. The epic incorporated heroic ballads sung to the lyre, and every part of it doubtless was intoned in some fashion even as late as classical times. Elegiac and iambic verse were also initially sung, accompanied by the aulos and the lyre respectively. Aeolian monody and Dorian choral poetry remained truly melic arts, choral song encompassing dance also as a regular constituent. Later centuries had no parallel for Greek melic poetry, which, as it has come down to us, is only too obviously a torso.

The drama too, derived from the cult of Dionysus, was sung to a great extent, incorporating both monodic and choral song, along with orchestics. Only with the new dithyramb of Phrynis and Timotheus did music begin to undergo a fateful and irreversible fractionation in which its unity was forever lost. The complete combination of poetry, melody, and dance, however, was the ideal type of music as well as the predominant type; and it must therefore be our point of reference in the study of both Greek music and Greek poetry. But we have not fully accounted for the connection of the musical arts unless we realize that their separation is often more apparent than actual. Performance intermediate between speech and song was undoubtedly prevalent, in the form of chant or recitative or intonation, and the Greek language was in any event remarkably physical and measured. It could never lose an inherent music which was characterized by precisely defined durations.

The comparison of choral poetry to a mosaic has justly gained a certain currency:[15] the Greek syllables were like unalterable stone tiles which are assembled contiguously in intricate successions of length. In sharp contrast is the modern fabrication of poetry out of the aura of feeling and fancy that surrounds words: the result here is an intangible play of meanings supported by the punctuation of accented points in a pattern made up of silence as well as sound. If Greek poetry was much more physical, it had its place appropriately in a literature which, even after the coming of prose, was conceived for oral delivery and almost always heard rather than read. Each tone also was ideally coupled to a gesture; the melody was mirrored in bodily motion. The very term *choros* meant round dance with song, and the concrete nature of Greek music was revealed even in the fundamental units of rhythm, which were not abstract durations of given length, but were defined as steps and syllables—as physical facts or events. But still more fundamental than physical motion was the word; Greek music worthy of the name necessarily involved language. Wordless music was regarded as inferior, and instrumental performance can be distinguished as *techne* (which is in no wise different from craft since it lacks imitative capacity) from the more elevated *mousike* (which generally designates vocal music).

There can be no doubt that the union of melody with word and gesture produced an art of extraordinary definition, especially since the uniting factor, rhythm, was identical in all three components; there was not a complex interplay of three patterns, but a single rhythmic expression, which was apparently the most important aspect of Greek music. Nor was this rhythm in itself a layered construction, as in the rhythm of an eighteenth- or nineteenth-century melody, where the sounded pattern is heard against an implied but inaudible measured background. And the unity of Greek rhythm was further solidified by unison singing and "unison" dancing; thus Greek music is comparable to Greek statuary and architecture in that it possessed a remarkably definite physical nature.

The imitative nature of music, its unified concreteness, and its ethical force are all importantly interrelated, and it is only through an awareness of their interconnection that we can secure an insight into the musical ethics of antiquity. If the basic task of music is the production of a likeness, for example, it is understandable that melody must not be separated from words, for then its imitative capacity would decrease and its meaning would become vague. Also, it is the power of music to imitate virtue that explains its capacity to influence and mold character. Thus the conception of imitation acts as an intermediary between the concrete nature of music and its ethical effects, and undertakes to explain how the one can bring about the other. This whole circle of notions is not so restrictive a characterization of art as it might seem; for one thing, the Greek concept of imitation actually includes components of formative activity and of the synthesis or simulation of appearance apart from reference to a model. But even if we take mimesis in its specifically imitative sense, it is apparent that the matter to be imitated can be very diverse, extending from visual objects to character and even to the idea of virtue itself rather than its particular manifestations. The imitation of character by music has a very definite sense in the literal imitation of the speech and behavior of a person by means of vocal music and gesture, particularly in the portrayal of character in drama; indeed we have seen that musical pantomime, representation through one's own person, was very probably what mimesis originally designated. This is as concrete as or really more concrete than imitation in sculpture and painting.

Greek music was an imitation, however, less of visual appearance than of disposition or temperamental nature, expressed most typically in measured language and tone. Yet by virtue of a rapprochement between musical theory and harmonic metaphysics, it also enjoyed the privilege unique among the arts of imitating divine and ideal order; and as a manifestation of this order it is capable in Plato's *Timaeus* of leading man to virtue and knowledge as directly as the more literally conceived imitations of the *Republic* are able to inculcate the more specific virtues of valor and temperance. Music in the *Timaeus* is thought of as a purely tonal art; [16] all that matters is its ability to reflect the abstract values of noetic harmony; its slight imitative capacity in the absence of words and physical gesture has ceased to be of interest. Partly as a result of the diversified nature of musical imitation, the scope of the ethical aspects of music is no less impressive than the vast variety of Greek harmonic conceptions; it ranges from medical cures to an influence on the feelings, from the precept and moral example contained in sung words to the most pervasive and powerful effects on behavior and character.

Throughout the gradual redirection of Greek ideals from the physical to the intellectual, from the hero in combat to the philosopher and orator, poetry and music continued to occupy a position of the utmost importance both in formal education and in the various educative occasions of life.[17] The breadth and variety of its ethical effects seemed to endow music with value for every task. Even apart from the question of imitation, instruction in music has always been an essential part of an aristocratic ethic; from Homer to the European Renaissance, instrumental performance and song and dance have been indispensable accomplishments of the knight and the courtier; they are part of the whole aristocratic pattern of life.

The ritual observances of the knightly culture depicted by Homer made use of religious choral dance-songs, but ethical values can be found also in the individual dancing and singing and lyre playing that served as entertainment, for prominent in this secular sphere was the rehearsal in song of great military exploits. Singing such heroic narrations was a private pastime of Achilles, and there can be no doubt of their moral influence. We know also of the ceremonial music at funeral games, which in an ethical respect would appear to stand somewhere between the religious paean and the heroic ballad. The description in the *Iliad* of specifically educational activities in the case of the tutors Chiron and Phoenix supplements the general picture: education revolved around courtly accomplishments, which included training in song and dance and lyre playing as prominent features, and around the heroic deed, which was inspired by great models of the past enshrined in song.

It is this ideal of glory achieved by valor which was central in the life of the Homeric noble, and which was fostered by the *Iliad* and the *Odyssey* themselves in their long history as the fundaments of Greek education. The events of the *Iliad* itself look back to still older prototypes; this is the heart of the process through which the culture secures continuity; and very much as the actual educational use of the heroic ballad is described in the epic, so the epics in turn, originally themselves sung, became the examples furnishing moral inspiration to successive generations. Also, the glory to which the hero aspires and for which he is willing to sacrifice his life is really a musical one, for it consists in the poetic celebration that immortalizes his deed. Of this again the *Iliad* both relates examples and is itself the greatest example. Thus in the Homeric world, music and poetry have their highest function in the glorification of the hero and in an education that is based on this. And they employ an appropriate educational method, for by lending glory to some past exploit they turn it into an ideal of action and thus arouse the very competitive spirit that impels the hero to excel in battle.

The ethical functions of the Homeric epic were time and again adopted and modified by later Greek poetry, and the ideals it expressed never ceased to be an inspiration. An educative intent became common, manifested in a protreptic or admonitory tone and associated with the direct address of the poem to a particular person. The catalogue of maxims was a characteristic poetic genre. Most important of all was the continual concern with ideals and virtue, with the expression of the highest values of the poet and his culture. On occasion this took the form of a detailed code of behavior. Hesiod's *Works and Days* represents an early transformation of the epic in which the form is explicitly didactic, and the concern is with the virtues of work and justice, values not of the aristocracy but of the Boeotian peasantry. An explicit moral intention became a conspicuous feature of the philosophic epic also, here connected with metaphysical truth. It is this whole poetic tradition that Socrates and Plato revitalize, and in their critical inspection of the nature of virtue, they logically review all the specific ideals of the poets. To the ethical influence that poetry exerts through its meaning, however, we must add its ability to reinforce the values that inhere primarily in a situation rather than in the words themselves; the occasion of performance takes on increased significance and moral influence.

The elegiac poetry of Tyrtaeus advanced a changed ideal of heroism that applied to the soldier of Sparta in the seventh century B.C. Every warrior in the ranks became a hero, not only the great individual engaged in single combat, and the goal was service to the community: the glory of the polis supplanted personal glory. At the same time, the powerful effects of the aulos and the marching-song were put to use in military music. In addition, music became an event of competitive games, alongside athletics, and in this way it provided a means of achieving that individual glory no longer a dominant factor in battle, or at least a means of combining personal and civic fame. Most important of all, musical ceremonies and festivals united the polis in a truly common religious experience.

With Alcman, toward the end of the seventh century, choral poetry became the characteristic musical expression of Sparta. Like the elegy, however, which originated in Ionia but in the work of Tyrtaeus and Solon and Theognis spread to all of Greece, Dorian communal poetry was by no means confined to Laconia, but was found also in Sicily, Boeotia, Ionia, and Athens. But as contrasted with the elegy, which taught by precept, and with the iambic, which made use of maxim, fable, satire, and invective, choral poetry taught largely by participation. Spartan festivals furnished the occasions for a wide variety of dance-songs devoted to specific deities and ranging

from solemn processions to banter. Participation in any choral poetry meant dedication to a tradition, and could hardly remain without a strong ethical effect. Taken over from the epic was the typical
religious-social function of praise, which made choral poetry characteristically hymnlike in nature. Praise could easily encompass com-
memoration of the dead or patriotic exhortation; it tended to absorb
every social and ethical value. That it was a universal theme can be
clearly seen in the Hellenistic division of melic poetry into three
types, all of them concerned with praise and differing only in their
objects: gods, gods and men, and men respectively, a classification
anticipated in the musical discussion of Plato's *Laws*. Starting in the
middle of the sixth century, Spartan education assumed the form
that became so well known and influential in later times; it became
less intellectual, more strictly military, and increasingly resistant to
change. Important in the subsequent history of musical influences
are the military use of music for its directly stimulating effect, and
the standardization of repertory that guarded traditional social and
military values.

In contrast to the strong collectivism in Sparta, Greek culture
elsewhere preserved much of the individualistic standards of older
times. The gnomic elegies of Theognis, for example, which were
sung at symposia, conveyed explicit moral principles of aristocratic
behavior. And up to the time of Plato, education was conducted
very little in formal schools, but was based on an individual relationship, the love between master and pupil, which dominated the
philosophic academy as well as private tutoring. In this lay its
strength and perhaps the ultimate reason for its vast influence on the
course of educational history; instead of being a relatively superficial
matter of imparting knowledge, it was a fundamentally moral undertaking of cultivating and molding character, of fashioning the
person in accordance with a particular way of life.

In such a framework the importance of music becomes more
readily understandable. Before schools were public, they were for

centuries societies of the elect, each pupil bound by personal ties to the master. Music took its part in a leisured and aristocratic life; but still more important was its role in ritual, which involved the age-old connection of music with knowledge, and more especially, with wisdom (which contains an ethical component). The philosophic school was dedicated to music, or we can equally well say, to culture. In the activities of the Pythagorean brotherhood, as we have indicated, music may very well have displayed the full variety of its ethical powers, many of them without any basis in imitation; it was a component of ritual, a medical purification of the soul, and even—in the form of theoretic and scientific study—a key to metaphysical knowledge; it was studied, that is, for directly philosophical and religious reasons, and not only employed in sonorous form for more palpable influences on health and piety. In the case of Sappho's school in Lesbos, there was continual use of music in periodic ritual and ceremony; and instruction in lyre playing, singing, and dance was an important part of the curriculum. This implies a pervasive ethical influence; but the Sapphic fragments not only provide glimpses of the place of music in the school of the poetess: they are remnants of a potent art which was itself music and which brought to Greek consciousness many subtle shades of subjective experience. In this way, her poems possessed a broad educational value that extended far beyond her immediate circle.

But if the public nature of Spartan education contrasts with the aristocratic Greek tradition of private tutoring, another contrast is provided by Athenian education of the earlier fifth century, for this was civilian rather than military. But neither this significant change nor the growth of democracy radically affected the persistence of aristocratic values. These proved to be compatible with the ideal of social justice which the poetry of Solon had long before envisaged as a counterpart of the balanced order of nature, and now valor and glory were retained in a civilian and democratic setting simply by transferring them from the battlefield to athletics. As a result, sport took on a new intensity, and the celebration of victory in the various games, especially as we see it in the epinicia of Pindar, was of the highest dignity and impressiveness. But at the same time, the process of democratization presented a problem. Athletics were to a great extent open to all, and in the public school, which grew up side by side with individual education, aristocratic ideals and curricula were similarly adopted for common use. The outcome was a serious controversy, for the belief did not die that culture was a restricted phenomenon and education necessarily a selective matter. In any event, music retained its historical ethical role and its commanding status. As far as intellectual education was concerned—that is, apart from gymnastics—the chief mark of a cultivated man was the ability to sing and dance and play the lyre.

Outside the formal education of the schools, choral poetry continued to exert its powerful moral influence, especially in Sparta, while the drinking party, highly organized and probably the most important institution of Greek cultural life, provided a more restricted aristocratic class with training that was almost exclusively moral and almost exclusively musical. Dancing and performances on lyre and aulos were secondary to the scolion, in which each guest sang in his turn. A knowledge of poetry that extended from epic to lyric was a presupposition of such gatherings: Homer and Tyrtaeus and Solon and Theognis furnished an extremely comprehensive moral cultivation, in which the explicit teachings of elegiac poetry were probably of chief importance. It was the symposium that was mainly responsible for the preservation of an aristocratic ethic. Most importantly, the older choral poetry of Stesichorus, Alcman, Simonides, and Pindar—known to the cultivated man through his participation in choral song—came to be performed monodically, so that the symposium incorporated the ideals of civic education and ensured the vitality and continuity of the musical tradition of liberal studies.

Prior to the Sophists and Socrates, Greek education was in general more physical and moral than it was intellectual, and it consequently made use more of actual music than of music as a theoretic and philosophic study. As a reflection of aristocratic ideals, it really never lost its liberal interests and its distrust of occupational training, and even when the supreme goal of military prowess and valor was abandoned, it aimed at cultivation for a leisured way of life compounded of sport and intellectual pleasures, with political activity as the typical serious pursuit.

But in the later fifth century, education took on a more purely intellectual intensity and a new ideal of wisdom. The scientific and philosophic aspects of music grew in importance alongside practical music and for the most part unrelated to it. In this change, the philosopher supplanted the poet as an educator, and we can consequently see a particular logic in Plato's designation of philosophy as the highest music. But as philosophy was music in an abstract sense more than an actual one, so the educational ideal it advocated was more one of musical science than of practical music. The stress on intellectual education did not necessarily involve a discard of ethical cultivation, however, but only a change in standards. Practical music was reinterpreted as a preparation for the rational training that came afterward, although its direct social and moral values were not overlooked. Much of the new outlook had been anticipated long before by Xenophanes: he turned to poetry rather than prose as a philosophic medium; he recited at symposia, thus usurping the position of the poets; he took direct issue with Homer in much the terms Plato did, criticizing him as immoral; and he advanced an intellectual rather than a physical ideal.

More subtly, Plato reduces gymnastics to a matter affecting the soul rather than the body; [18] but he by no means loses sight of their inherent values, and seeks only to turn them back to their older significance as preparation for battle rather than for victory in athletic competition. Almost symbolically, in the *Symposium,* he explicitly relegates music to the category of entertainment,[19] while the time of the company is spent in the higher activity of philosophical discussion, the new and superior kind of music. This is doubtless a conscious depiction of new educational ideals, which Plato was quite ready to view from a musical standpoint. With the Sophists, relativism could easily lead to a discard of music as an ethical force; in the world of dialectics and oratory that they created it was to be retained only as an emotional and technical aid to the speaker. But the renewed faith of Socrates and Plato in an absolute moral standard brought with it a belief in the older ethical values of music and in musical value in general. Yet the nature of music was changing, and as the old unity fell apart the educational ideals and curriculum based on it changed also; political and social changes were a counterpart—or a result, as Damon and Plato believed; the logical outcome was the destruction of the polis and the growth of the cosmopolitan city, a process accompanied by an equivalent disruption of music. In attempting to reinterpret and preserve the older ideals, Plato found himself opposed to what was actually a more progressive attitude, for philosophy fought with rhetoric over the educational leadership abandoned by music, and rhetoric frankly accepted the musical disintegration and the new intellectual specialization, replacing universality with versatility.

In any event, the musical-poetic tradition reveals that the educative function of music exists in poetry of whatever type, although the precise function varies with the genre. The teaching values of gnomic verse are there for all to see, but even the philosophic epic evolved from the didactic epic, and traces of its origin are still evident in so late a descendant as Lucretius. The motif of moral instruction, intimately allied to music, runs through the entire history of Greek poetry and philosophy, and indeed through all the literature of antiquity. In its direct address to a single individual, the prose protreptic continues the manner of didactic and moral poetry; philosophy has already adopted the device in Empedocles' time, and with Isocrates the genre becomes established. The *Epinomis* (intended as a final section of Plato's *Laws*), Aristotle's *Protrepticus,*

Cicero's *Hortensius,* Boethius' *Consolation,* and the patristic "Exhortation" are outstanding examples. But vastly more impressive than the explicit exhortation is the Platonic dialogue itself, with its powerful inspirational effect.

The education of Greece was the high ethical purpose that philosophy carried over from poetry, and if Homer was the teacher of Greece, Plato became the teacher of the West. But in its superior realization of this purpose, philosophy directed upon poetry not gratitude but criticism. For poetry did not deal in abstract argument; it made use of feelings and the concrete instance; it was fallible in morality and naive in the discernment of truth. Furthermore poetry was degenerating, in Plato's opinion; it had lost sight of its social mission, while those participating in it became effeminate and depraved. The actors in Athenian tragedy stood on a plane vastly inferior to that of the participants in Dorian choral dance. It was symptomatic that the aulos had taken on a new popularity, and ornate musical styles had appeared, in conjunction with virtuosity and purely instrumental music.[20] Imitation ran riot, with attempted duplications of the sounds of nature and animals and various musical instruments; the citharoedic singer imitated the quavering excitement of the aulos; modulation, chromaticism, and a mixture and confusion of styles accompanied a continuous search for novel effects, and music was dedicated to senseless pleasure and applause.

The ethical values of poetry became an important issue in the case of Athenian tragedy, and indeed were the core of the controversy over the relative merits of Aeschylus and Euripides. In the *Frogs* of Aristophanes, Aeschylus rehearses the traditional moral and social function of the poet: "Those are the subjects that poets should use. Note how useful, even from remotest times, the poets of noble thought have been! Orpheus taught us the mystic rites and the horrid nature of murder; Musaeus, the healing of ailments and the oracles; Hesiod, the tilling of the soil and the times for delving and harvest. And does not divine Homer owe his immortal glory to his noble teachings? Is it not he who taught the warlike virtues, the art of fighting and of carrying arms?"[21] And in answer to a question about the truth of a story used by Euripides, he says, "No, the story is true enough; but the poet should hide what is vile and not produce nor represent it on the stage. The schoolmaster teaches little children and the poet men of riper age. We must only display what is good."[22] Truth is not a sufficient standard of poetic value, then, a concept that Plato develops in detail.

It is clear at the close of the play that Aeschylus carries the day precisely by virtue of his social role. Aristophanes takes the occasion to criticize Socrates also, whom he treats as the representative of rhetoric, for engaging in idle talk, that is, in an activity not socially useful. Even the medical power of music is wielded by Aeschylus, as it is by Musaeus, in the passage cited above. "Let us beware of jabbering with Socrates," the chorus sings, "and of disdaining the sublime notes of the tragic Muse. To pass an idle life reeling off grandiloquent speeches and foolish quibbles, is the part of a madman."[23] And Pluto continues: "Farewell, Aeschylus! Go back to earth and may your noble precepts both save our city and cure the mad; there are such, a many of them!"[24] In the *Clouds,* Aristophanes paints a vivid picture of the immoral and outrageous results of sophistical education; yet however mistaken it may be in its attribution to Socrates and however ludicrously distorted, it really has a foundation of truth in the dangerous ethical relativism of the Sophists.[25] As a poet, Aristophanes will naturally prefer poetry to rhetoric, but his true motives go beyond this, as we can see in his detailed criticism of Euripides; he is not only the greatest of craftsmen, but a defender and representative of the high ethical mission of his art.

Pindar, who was a contemporary of Aeschylus and, with Theognis, the chief champion of the great aristocratic tradition, gives us our deepest insight into the cultural force of music in a commemorative context. Not only are his odes themselves music, actually serving the high purpose to which choral dance was dedicated, but they often explicitly describe music in its central religious and social function. In the twelfth Pythian Ode we are fortunate to possess an epinicion honoring an aulos player; the Pythian games included music as a field of competition. The poem is a rich tapestry of meanings, wonderfully interwoven.[26] There is an invocation to the Greek colony of Agrigentum, in Sicily, for this is the home of the victor, Midas. Then the myth of Athena's invention of the aulos is told: how Perseus beheaded Medusa, and how after Athena had freed him from his toil she heard the mournful cries of Medusa's sisters and invented the "polycephalous melody" in imitation of them. Breath flows through the aulos reed, mirroring the action of the human voice. The reed has grown in a holy region near the city of Orchomenos, which is known for its beautiful round dances; thus it has always looked upon dancing as it is doing on this occasion. There is a moral also: as it always has in the past, success comes only with effort and with divine aid.

Music has a remarkably elaborate significance in the ode; it permeates every value, ennobling hero, city, land, ritual, and tradition. The aulos is physically part of the ceremony of celebration, but it is also discussed in the poem itself, and its reed has grown in the ground on which the dance takes place. And the victor's glory is really the glory of the city, but it is given still deeper meaning by the divine origin of the instrument and the melody-type: Midas is something like the priest of a specific musical ritual. Choral dance is basically religious music, and thus naturally encompasses both myth and moral teaching. In all the longer odes myth occupies the central part, tied somehow to the victorious occasion, either to the hero, to his family, or to his city and its particular gods and heroes. It is really only in this reference to current occasions and places that the epinicia differ from the dithyrambs. Thus both music and life are given depth and meaning; they are viewed as continuous with a sacred tradition extending into a divine past.

It becomes especially evident here that the ethical force of music derives from its religious and social nature, which is manifested both in its ritual importance and in its public and patriotic functions. Choral song was the heart of the Pythian games, and the drama an essential feature of the Dionysian festivals. Furthermore, in its content, Greek literature almost always has a social orientation; the isolated individual, like the autonomy of art, hardly had a meaning. Consequently the poet was not just a national hero as an artist, but was regarded literally as a teacher and leader, and at times as a prophet, a role emphasized by the divine nature of musical inspiration. Plato is not simply being contentious when he demands an active political or social career from the poet before he will consider him a worthwhile member of society.[27] An outstanding example of the poet as a leader—and of the practical import of morality in poetry—is that of Solon, the great statesman of Athens; and it is obvious that the numerous tales of poets in the guise of rulers and peacemakers, like the stories of Sparta's repeated recourse to musicians in hours of need, cannot be totally without foundation. Thus when philosophy and oratory laid claim to teaching and to leadership, they could do so only in a conscious attempt to fill the role of poetry. Plato's dispute with the poets and the rhetoricians revolves to no small extent around the educational value of these rival pursuits, although, to be sure, possessing both poetic genius and an incredible mastery of rhetoric, he is easily able to carry off the victory.

But music does not merely present conceptual material to the intellect; it molds character more directly in the psychological impact of its rhythm and meter and melody, and more forcefully still in the fact that choral dance-song compels participation, calling for musical performers who also must take part in a ceremonial experience. This is in particular the Dorian tradition of music, exemplified by Sparta; it is the great Grecian ideal that Plato unhesitatingly adopts. Compared with it all other varieties of art shrink to insig-

nificance: the tragedians have come to pander to the public, instrumental virtuosity is directed solely to pleasure, the monodists are
lascivious, art in general is false and corrupting.

There can be no doubt that every element of music contributed its
share to the whole ethical quality.[28] The moral content of the
words was reinforced by bodily movements, by meter and melody of
the same quality and character, and by an appropriate tempo. Even
in isolation, each component would have something of the same
nature as the whole, and would express the same feeling and have the
same effect, albeit in less precise and powerful form. What remains
of Greek music permits us to verify this only for meter; melody and
gesture have disappeared with hardly a trace. Only theoretical discussion of musical ethos opens to us some knowledge of the specific
capabilities of various scales and types of melody, dance, and
rhythm. But in the application of meter to reflect the moral nature
of ideas we have a storehouse of practice that helps to round out
technical and aesthetic discussion; and it becomes clear that each
variety of meter has its own ethical nature which helped it to define
a particular genre of poetry to begin with, so that poetry and drama
slowly develop a stock of moral and expressive values. The ethos of
meter becomes particularly prominent when the nature of the poetic
genre permits combinations of different metrical types or the construction of new ones, as is conspicuously the case in dramatic composition, which is not only analogous to panharmonic music but
liable to the same Platonic criticism of playing a wanton game with
human feelings rather than inculcating the pattern of officially approved virtue. Dochmiac meter had an effect of anxiety or despair,
anapaestic one of dignity, the paeonic was excited, the epitrite grave.
Some meters were obviously capable of a variety of effects, even apart
from tempo, which of course would always be an influential factor.
Also, metrical composition, like melodic, could involve complex and
individual constructions for each work, as it does in Pindar. The
musical genius of the composer might arrange long and short sylla-

bles and syncopations without the guidance of theory, but in quite the same way as it arranged the constituent pitches and intervals in a melody.

Both the technical theory of musical ethics and its general moral and social philosophy were formulated toward the middle of the fifth century B.C. by Damon, an Athenian philosopher and musical theorist.[29] This influential man was a pupil of the Sophist Prodicus, an adviser of Pericles, and a teacher of Socrates, but in spite of his importance, our knowledge of his ideas is due almost exclusively to fragments of an oration, his *Areopagiticus,* and to several references to him by Socrates and Plato, who speak of him with the greatest respect. The discovery and analytical application of the metrical foot seem to have been his work, as well as contributions to the system of the *harmoniai.* Ethically he was concerned with the effects of various rhythmic and melodic patterns upon human nature, and set up typologies of rhythms, modes, and characters. He was the leading authority in the field of the specific moral effects of music, maintaining also that there was an indissoluble connection between music and society, so that musical changes inevitably entailed legal ones. The thesis of his oration was undoubtedly that the guardianship of good law and good order should remain as the function of the Areopagus, the oldest and most distinguished of the Athenian tribunals, and that this function was best discharged through music, which in affecting the human soul could similarly affect the soul of the state—its laws and political constitution.

When Athenian philosophy concerned itself with the teaching of virtue, it naturally had to come to terms with traditional and current conceptions of education, which were represented chiefly by the Sophists. Training in music and gymnastics was prescribed by law,[30] and the great Sophist Protagoras, in contrast to the later representatives of his profession, believed in the value and strength of musical influences. In the dialogue of Plato named for him, Protagoras is interested in demonstrating that virtue can be taught, and

he appropriately recounts the whole customary course of education.[31] He describes epic poetry's admonitions, praises, and encomia
of ancient famous men which the child must learn by heart so that
he may imitate or emulate them and desire to become like them.
And he discusses also how the child learns lyric poetry and its
accompaniment by the lyre, which makes the *harmoniai* and
rhythms familiar to his soul, thus teaching him to be more gentle,
harmonious, and rhythmical. Then gymnastics are used to
strengthen his body, so that it may better minister to his virtuous
mind.

Education based on music and gymnastics, the one for the soul
and the other for the body, is discussed at length in Books II and III
of the *Republic* in connection with the guardians of the state.
Music should precede gymnastics, for children can be told stories
before they are ready for physical training. (This is a point that
could have no more apt illustration than the time-honored use of
nursery songs and rhymes and dances.) The importance of fashioning the mind is such that only authorized tales are to be used. Their
fundamental requirement is ethical value; it is for this reason that
truth is essential, while falsehood is admissible—provided it has a
beneficial moral influence—only in the sense of fiction. In every aspect of music the preservation of social and moral values demands
censorhip and control. The content of epic poetry must not lead to
fear of death and so prevent the development of courage; it must
not tell of the weeping of famous men; nor must the gods be
represented as lamenting. Similarly neither worthy persons nor the
gods should be depicted as overcome by laughter. Instead temperance is to be represented, with respect both to properly obedient
behavior and to self-control in sensuous pleasures. Famous deeds of
endurance are also fit subject matter. Disapproved are descriptions
of heroes or gods as receivers of gifts or lovers of money. Poets are
guilty of impiety if they depict gods as authors of evil or heroes as
no better than ordinary men.

As far as the representation of men is concerned, poets must not tell us that the wicked are often happy and the good miserable, or that injustice is profitable when undetected, or that justice is no more than one man's loss and another man's gain, for all these ideas are false. The content of poetry, then, Plato implies, waits upon philosophy and the knowledge of truth.

Like subject matter, style too is controlled. Imitations in poetry of natural sounds and events or of men are to be carefully restricted. Completely imitative genres, such as comedy and tragedy, are prohibited, while lyric poetry and the dithyramb, in which the rhapsodist voices only the poet's words, are approved. The mixed style of epic poetry is acceptable, for it is largely narrative, and where men are imitated and the bard must momentarily become an actor, his imitation is of an elevated and serious character quite in keeping with the prevailing tone of the narration. Thus, as Plato points out, the rhythm and harmony can remain unified, and there need be no mixture or sudden changes of quality.

Clearly imitation is conceived throughout the discussion in the original and particular sense of personal dramatic representation. When he discusses harmonies and rhythms, Plato specifically permits only those that are appropriate to imitations of virtue as revealed in action and speech. The acceptable modes are the Dorian and the Phrygian, which imitate temperance and courage respectively; in the *Statesman* the weaving together of these two virtues is seen as the task of the ruler. The other modes—the sorrowful ones and the relaxed—are prohibited. Restrictions on the use of musical instruments and rhythms express the same attitude. If imitations of virtue are a force for virtue, then imitations of vice are destructive. Not only debilitating modes are to be excluded, but the aulos as well, and certain rhythms that are to be determined with the help of experts. Musical imitations must also be consistent and clear. Instrumental music is obviously deficient in respect of clarity, as is any separation of music into its component arts. The modes and the rhythms subserve the whole style, which expresses the soul. Thus primarily, style in art is to be simple in accordance with the beauty of nature itself; it is to mirror the most beautiful harmony of all, that of body and soul. Complex panharmonic music is the counterpart of a luxurious life. A basic requirement for the musician, then, is that he know the various forms of virtue and vice; he cannot imitate moral nature successfully if he is unfamiliar with his model.

Finally, this music is to be blended with gymnastics that are simple and good like itself, so that the two may produce the desired qualities of soul. Gymnastics and music do not simply act on body and soul respectively, for gymnastics really use the body as an instrument to reach the soul. Thus gymnastics affect the spirited part of the soul and music its rational or philosophic part. An excess in either is bad, leading on the one hand to hardness and on the other to softness. The true musician, taking the word "musician" now in the characteristically abstract sense it acquires in Greece, will know how to combine the two and to apply them to the individual soul. Music and gymnastics will harmonize reason and spirit, and these principles together will in turn control desire, so that the harmony of the three principles of the soul and the harmony of soul and body are both due to the ethical influence of the two major divisions of education.

In Plato's view of human nature and music there is a persistent dual scheme of virtue which figures prominently in the *Republic,* the *Laws,* and the *Statesman:* that of war and peace, of courage and moderation, of spirit and reason. Accordingly we can take the two classes of rhythm he will permit, or the Phrygian and Dorian modes, as respectively efficacious in the two spheres, and the gymnastic component of education, acting through the body on the spirited part of the soul, will have an alternative in the cultivation of valor by means of Phrygian melodies. Thus Dorian and Phrygian will affect different parts of the soul, an odd result which is confirmed by the fact that the *Timaeus* gives a Dorian structure to the rational part of the soul.

What is actually the reason for the restrictions Plato places on the imitative style? Why does he have a fear of imitation and of its power for evil? His attitude is consistent with his social goals, and it is comprehensive, applying to both performers and auditors.

The imitator, and especially the actor, who imitates with his own person, will come to resemble that which is imitated; this is a danger that also threatens the listener and the spectator.[32] What is more, the imitation of a variety of models produces in itself an effeminate lack of definition in the imitator and evidently in the listener as well. Also art indulges the feelings, a process in which Plato, unlike Aristotle, generally sees no cathartic value, although exception must be made in the case of his recognition of the emotional purification brought about by orgiastic rite.[33] The emotions require control, but art stimulates them instead, and to make matters worse, it does so on the basis of a spurious cause: the sadness we feel in viewing the representation of a tragic event is pernicious because it is a response to a counterfeit.[34] Finally the matter of imitation is related to the place of specialization in the ideal society. No man can do many things well; and particularly in the case of the guardians of the state, optimum performance is a vital requirement for the welfare and safety of all. If they were to practice imitations of cowardice, for example, or even to be exposed as listeners to the melodies and rhythms that are part of such representations, incalculable harm might be done through the dissipation of their abilities as well as the direct cancellation of courage.

In determining the effect of art, the mode of imitation is apparently as important as the presented subject matter. The argument of Books II and III of the *Republic* looks upon imitation as pantomime, as a particular style of poetry or music; but in the general context of Plato's thought imitation is the distinguishing characteristic of all art, or at least of all fine art. Thus its effects and dangers are not restricted to drama, and Plato can logically accept other poetic styles not because they are not imitative, but because they are imitative in a different and less harmful way. Their true advantage is that the object of imitation remains the same throughout, but this object—like that of any imitation—must be morally acceptable. The potency of imitation is particularly great in music because musical imitations extend most directly and immediately to character and the soul.[35]

It is important to distinguish the views of good and bad art which are found in both the *Republic* and the *Laws* from the universal condemnation of art contained in Book X of the *Republic*. In the ethical theory of aesthetics of the *Republic* (Books II and III), imitation is judged chiefly by the virtue of its object, and in the similar theory of the *Laws* (Books II and VII), chiefly by its fidelity to this object; but in the hostile view of Book X of the *Republic*, the object of imitation is of no importance: imitation as such is an exercise of the emotions without legitimate cause and consequently leads to lack of emotional control, both because it strengthens the feelings and because reason is set aside in the response. Also, whether it is accurate or not, it is twice removed from truth; metaphysically regarded, and with reality residing in the Ideas, it is a copy of a copy. But we may take this as an incomplete picture, especially from the point of view of ethics. It is certainly sounder psychologically and socially to rely on the strengthening of desirable feelings and beliefs by habit.[36] And as far as music is concerned, ceremony furnishes a concrete setting for the imitation that offsets its removal from truth. Actually music is less an imitation of a model than a new event with adumbrations of historical precedent.

The ethical role of music is not exhausted by the education of the guardians; still further procedures are outlined in the *Republic* (Book VII) for a higher and more selective education that is intended in particular for the rulers of society.[37] Now Plato goes beyond the moral qualities of courage and temperance and harmony of the soul to an education for the highest goal of man, the pursuit of philosophy, which involves the gradual transcendence of sensory experience. He thus turns from objects and their images to the abstractions of science and dialectic, although in his conception of education these subjects could not be known if a favorable predisposition toward them in the character of the learner had not been gradually built up earlier through music.

Here is the philosophic confirmation, however, if not the beginning, of that fateful separation of art and science, of lower and higher education, which drove music out of advanced studies altogether, keeping only its name as an alternative description for theoretic disciplines such as harmonics and rhythmics. As it is centuries later in the march of Hegel's Spirit, art is superseded by pure thought, which can directly know the Ideas. These eternal entities may derive their rational character from the Being of Parmenides, but they preserve as well something of the objectivity of the Olympian gods, and similarly call for admiration and almost religious veneration. Their conception even contains traces of a visual origin; the *Epinomis* significantly places astronomy at the summit of higher education, and identifies divinity with the visible heavens. In any event, education for philosophy takes on the greatest moral import; the ultimate goal is the Good, and this end, too, music in its most general sense is able to subserve. The Ideas are reached by dialectic, which proceeds by reason alone, but the point of departure is sense and the route leads through harmonic theory.

The disciplines that have the preparatory function of freeing man from the confusions of sense are the sister sciences of Archytas: arithmetic, geometry, astronomy, and music. We have seen that these were traditional subjects of study,[38] undoubtedly of Pythagorean origin; the *Protagoras* tells us that the Sophists retaught them, the *Theaetetus* mentions them as the studies that go to make an educated man, and they again make up the curriculum of the *Laws,* with the noteworthy difference that actual music takes the place of harmonics (for the other disciplines Plato simply acknowledges the existence of a popular or nonscientific aspect).

At the end of the *Laws,* however, as we have mentioned, music as harmonics is considered to be a subject related to all higher studies, and in the *Epinomis,* harmonics is treated only in this connection and omitted entirely as a separate discipline. Again in the *Lesser Hippias* the place of music is exceptional; arithmetic (especially its practical counterpart, calculation), geometry, and astronomy are mentioned among the numberless accomplishments of the boastful Sophist Hippias, and later on music is listed along with other subjects, but spoken of as rhythmics and harmonics and coupled with orthography.

The *Republic* considers the mathematical sciences to be preparatory to philosophy and political administration, but in the *Laws* and the *Epinomis* this motif is weaker; the *Epinomis* more or less equates the sciences with philosophy and thus emphasizes the self-sufficiency they apparently possess in the other dialogues. The *Republic* also introduces a fifth science, placing stereometry or solid geometry between geometry and astonomy for systematic reasons, although it obscures the significant symmetry of the Pythagorean scheme. Of each of the disciplines Plato stresses the abstract and ideal character; they are not concerned with practical use, nor with experienced objects at all. In the case of harmonics, it is not only a concern with actual tones that Plato discards, but also what he takes as the interest of the Pythagoreans—the study of harmonic numbers and proportions. Harmonics is to deal instead with the problem of why certain numbers are harmonic, the problem of the nature of harmony.

We have come a great distance from actual music, but we have by no means left ethical influence behind—only changed its character; harmonics is more than an ontological study: it contains its own kind of moral value. Sonorous music is a matter of habit and training;

it affects the nature of the guardians, making them harmonious and rhythmical. But it does not give them science; it contains nothing that will draw the soul from becoming to being, that will tend toward the highest good. This is certainly a sharp distinction between art and science, between a relatively mechanical process and a purely intellectual one, although without the preparation of the earlier training the later study would be fruitless. And just as music sets the tone for the concept of the lower education, so harmony is the typical representative of the higher. It is at any rate the last of the mathematical disciplines, and thus the most general of them, for the order is not arbitrary. Number is succeeded by plane figures, plane figures by solids, solids by the motion of solids, and this motion by the motion of sounds. While apart from the concept of cosmogonical succession the Pythagorean classification is a static analysis of being, the pedagogical and propaedeutic function together with the introduction of a fifth science transform the Platonic scheme into a dynamic ascent. At each step, abstraction is made from the sensory phenomena to principles.

Then, after the study of the interrelationship of the principles of all the disciplines, which is an investigation itself harmonic in nature, the ascent of dialectic begins. If we treat the *Republic* itself as an example, dialectic, too, is largely the study of harmony, in man and state and world. And when we are told that the preliminary sciences are the handmaids and helpers of dialectic, the intention seems to be not only that their help is preparatory, but also that they are continuous adjuncts. Again the *Republic* provides confirmation: much more than the proposal of a curriculum, it is an actual instance of the philosophical use of the principles of the preparatory disciplines; and the *Philebus* furnishes a still more striking illustration of the role that harmony can play in the dialectic advance toward the good.

The *Republic* describes the process of social dissolution in some detail,[39] incidentally providing an artistic balance to the earlier constructive discussion, and music is here shown as causal in a negative rather than a positive sense. Ignorance of the law governing human births will lead to inferior guardians, and their first failing will be in not taking care of the Muses, in neglecting music. As a result, future guardians will successively make other errors; social discord will spread in a cumulative fashion. It is interesting that Plato takes stock of the self-perpetuating nature of changes in music and society, whether they are beneficial or destructive; but of greater importance is the fact that the whole interdependence of education and the state is conceived in terms of harmony and music, and that the long discussion of social disintegration is introduced in these terms. The connection between sonorous music and the abstract notion of harmony makes the pertinence of value to harmony especially clear. Since the original cause of the social discord was a departure from the number regulating human births, the error actually starts in harmonics and then spreads to music and to social harmony.

In the *Laws*,[40] although Plato repeats many of his earlier musical theories, he also explores additional aspects of the ethical force of music, and in particular extends his program of education to include public festivals, all classes of society, and the very earliest stages of life, seeking even to revitalize the historic educational role of the symposium in connection with convivial gatherings and feasts. His orientation is now primarily psychological, and he is especially concerned with the nature of play and with the impulses giving rise to music. Young children cannot be quiet; their motions and their cries are the material of music, and these become rhythm and harmony through a musical sense that is given to man by the gods.

Thus Plato has recourse to a Homeric mode of expressing innate human capacities; in this late dialogue the philosopher's awareness of the values of tradition is especially apparent. Rejoicing is the more immediate origin of music, but it is associated most properly with festivals in honor of the gods. Plato projects an annual cycle of religious celebrations. In addition to honoring the gods, however, such ceremonies have an educational function. The gods join with man in musical celebration; they have not only endowed him with a musical sense, but have actually written particular songs for his use. Music is consequently sacred, and religious tradition becomes the basis of its influence.

In explaining creative musical ability by attributing songs to the gods, Plato is again consciously employing an older mode of thought in which the powers of the mind are taken as facts of divine action; but this conception is one he admires, and it artistically and logically reinforces the precise values he is stressing. Along with its psychological concern, the *Laws* reveals a great deal of historical and empirical sensitivity. Music should be consecrated as it is in Egypt, Plato holds; only then will it maintain social stability. In line with Damon's view that license in music will bring about changes in the laws of the state, Plato demands that there be no innovation; he fully believes that the decay of civic life in Athens, the military failure, and the loss of political stature are due to laxity and immorality in music. When once the true musical imitations have been determined by divine inspiration, any novelty or any departure from them will be a departure from virtue.

In this appropriate context, Plato again endorses only those melodies that express virtue, those that imitate the good. Such melodies are to be judged by the standard of truth, that is, by the accuracy of the imitation. The excellence of music is essentially identified with imitative fidelity; although workmanship, or beauty, is considered also, it is certainly of subordinate importance. This places a severe demand upon the judge of music, for he must know the good itself if he is to evaluate the accuracy of its musical imitation. The poet would be unsatisfactory, for he can judge only the beauty of an imitation, not its truth. Somewhat differently, the musical theories of the *Republic* characteristically stress the virtue of the judge rather than his knowledge, although exception must be made of the attitude of Book X. Thus in the earlier dialogue the judge must carefully avoid the actual experience of evil in his own education; in order to evaluate virtue he must be virtuous.[41] (In the education of the physician, on the other hand, the experience of illness should be included.)

But what is the status of pleasure in music? Only harmless amusement can take pleasure as a standard; music is an imitative art and is therefore subject to the standards of imitation. Thus pleasure can be no more than an accompanying charm, although it is valuable in making musical training attractive to the child. It depends actually on nature and habit, and consequently can attach to almost any object. It can be a criterion only when music is judged by the right people, by those who take pleasure in virtue, and not by the untutored populace. Training cannot completely change this situation and ensure that everyone will enjoy what is good, for it can alter only habit, not nature. Yet Plato has no wish to exclude pleasure; his effort is rather to retain an approved type by habituating the youth to the music of virtue.

Education in the *Laws* becomes something very like indoctrination, but it does so only as a result of the realization that indoctrination, whether for good or for ill, will exist in any event. The child is exposed to sights and sounds and ideas, and these can hardly be indifferent in moral constitution; some beliefs and feelings will be formed whether we will or no. This may not be made quite so explicit, but it plainly underlies Plato's theories. Music in particular, quite in keeping with the whole conservative and traditional standard of value, revives its archaic magical power, and becomes an enchantment practiced by the educator. There is generally evident in the dialogue a deliberate and rather unscrupulous determination to mold man in accordance with the envisaged social ideal; Plato is coolly shaping the material of his master art of education or his royal art of statesmanship. He gives special attention to the words that are sung, for young people, as he says, may be persuaded to believe anything. Poets must say that the good are happy, that injustice is unpleasant; all must sing that the holiest life is the happiest.

Certainly Plato is convinced that these statements are true; in many of his writings he undertakes to prove them. But they would in any event be useful lies. Philosophy is a vital matter that must necessarily govern the content of the curriculum. Society rests on beliefs and ideas. Socrates had been executed for not serving an older faith, and insisting upon the individuality of the soul, and it is now as though Plato wishes to turn the tables. Those who do not agree with him are more than intellectual rivals; they are heretics and disrupters of the social order. Those who do not worship the Ideas, which are the true philosophy, must be censored or banished if they cannot be made to see the light. The soul is immortal and the divine order is good; disagreement here would shake the foundations of the state.

Plato, of course, is quite cognizant of music that exists for amusement rather than for instruction, but he sets aside the realm of ethical indifference in the context of the *Republic* and gives it only brief mention in the *Laws*. In the urgent setting of a political utopia, harmless pleasure tends to appear either as emotional indulgence or as imitative of evil. More specifically, Plato decries musical excess as the ruin of the state; musical degeneracy leads to degeneracy in morals. The effect of bad music, he holds, is like the effect of bad company. Confusion, or a lack of definition, in the meaning of music is only a step removed from clearly vicious content.

Thus Plato again speaks against a separation of the component arts of music or an incongruity in their combination. Complexity (such as arises when an accompanying instrument does not simply duplicate the voice, for example) is another evil, closely related, for it will involve opposed tendencies which either mix different characters or obscure the imitation of virtue; in addition, it represents license and emotional depravity; virtue is inherently simple, and no true imitation of it can be complex. There is also the further practical criticism that complex music is discouragingly difficult to learn, and a crowded program of studies demands that time be used efficiently. The mixture of styles traditionally distinct is a similar defect; like innovation in general, it means the rejection of imitative truth in favor of pleasure, and thus spells social ruin.

As in the *Republic,* there are to be specific restrictions of musical content, which are the province of the statesman, not the poet, and for which the *Laws* itself (which appears to the Athenian protagonist to be quite like a poem and has even been divinely inspired) provides a model. Approved imitations are of two basic types: the Dance of War and the Dance of Peace; these correspond to the two accepted musical modes and types of rhythm in the *Republic,* which are also imitative of military and peaceful virtue, and they similarly correspond to the two kinds of melodies and rhythms discussed in the *Laws*—the one expressive of courage and the other of temperance—which are considered especially appropriate to men and women respectively. Behind the duality are the spirited and rational parts of the soul; the appetitive part must be considered to correspond to musical pleasure.

Specifically disapproved, like the aulos in the *Republic,* are the Bacchic dancing supposedly imitative of drunken men but actually without any meaning at all, and the dancing connected with mysteries and purifications—possibly representative of Orphic practice—for which there is again no clear or valuable object of imitation. Thus while the aulos was excluded in the *Republic* because of its character, orgiastic dancing—which is really liable to the same objection—is condemned along with ritual dancing because it is meaningless, and this is a reflection of a difference in emphasis in the evaluation of imitation, the *Republic* stressing virtue and the *Laws* truth.

Texts must be in praise of the gods or of heroes; they are regulated by a code which can be called a law about laws, because it is a law about a particular type of musical composition that has the same name (*nomos*) as a political statute. The traditional musical *nomoi,* which served the characteristic end of praise of the various gods, were defined ethically and technically;[42] they followed a sectionalized scheme and were doubtless melody-types.

This formulation according to law is mirrored in Plato's insistence upon the clear separation of different kinds of musical composition, and in view of the whole importance of music in his theory of society and education, the title of the *Laws* has a peculiar appropriateness. In an important passage that seeks to determine the nature of law by contrasting it with freedom, the discussion turns at once to music, for in music, it is maintained, lies the origin and foundation of both good order and lawlessness:

In the first place, let us speak of the laws about music—that is to say, such music as then existed—in order that we may trace the growth of the excess of freedom from the beginning. Now music was early divided among us into certain kinds and manners. One sort consisted of prayers to the gods, which were called hymns; and there was another and opposite sort called lamentations, and another termed paeans, and another, celebrating the birth of Dionysus, called, I believe, "dithyrambs." And they used the actual word "laws," or *nomoi,* for another kind of song; and to this they added the term "citharoedic." All these and others were duly distinguished, nor were the performers allowed to confuse one style of music with another. And the authority which determined and gave judgment, and punished the disobedient, was not expressed in a hiss, nor in the most unmusical shouts of the multitude, as in our days, nor in applause and clapping of hands. But the directors of public instruction insisted that the spectators should listen in silence to the end; and boys and their tutors, and the multitude in general, were kept quiet by a hint from the stick. Such was the good order which the multitude were willing to observe; they would never have dared to give judgment by noisy cries. And then, as time went on, the poets themselves introduced the reign of vulgar and lawless innovation. They were men of genius, but they had no perception of what is just and lawful in music; raging like Bacchanals and possessed with inordinate delights—mingling lamentations with hymns, and paeans with dithyrambs; imitating the sounds of the aulos on the lyre, and making one general confusion; ignorantly affirming that music has no truth, and, whether good or bad, can only be judged of rightly by the pleasure of the hearer. And by composing such licentious works, and adding to them words as licentious, they have inspired the multitude with lawlessness and boldness, and made them fancy that they can judge for themselves about melody and song. And in this way the theatres from being mute have become vocal, as though they had understanding of good and bad in music and poetry; and instead of an aristocracy, an evil sort of theatrocracy has grown up. For if the democracy which judged had only consisted of educated persons, no fatal harm would have been done; but in music there first arose the universal conceit of omniscience and general lawlessness; freedom came following afterwards, and men, fancying that they knew what they did not know, had no longer any fear, and the absence of fear begets shamelessness. For what is this shamelessness, which is so evil a thing, but the insolent refusal to regard the opinion of the better by reason of an over-daring sort of liberty? Consequent upon this freedom comes the other freedom, of disobedience to rulers; and then the attempt to escape the control and exhortation of father, mother, elders, and when near the end, the control of the laws also; and at the very end there is the contempt of oaths and pledges, and no regard at all for the gods—herein they exhibit and imitate the old so-called Titanic nature, and come to the same point as the Titans when they rebelled against God, leading a life of endless evils.[43]

Law is obviously similar to justice, as it is conceived in the *Republic;* both are characterized by regulated distinctions, the one in reflection of defined types of music, the other mirroring the specifically harmonic structure of the musical system.

The *Laws* depicts two types of gymnastics:[44] physical exercise pure and simple, which is devoted to the cultivation of the body, and dance, which as an imitation belongs to the sphere of choral art and has an ethical effect. Thus education based on gymnastics and music will become mostly musical, but the revised classification is hardly as important as the conceptions introduced in the *Republic,* where gymnastic is not only applied to the soul along with music, but also comprises with music a new and higher genus of noetic music which consists in the harmonic application of the two arts. Plato is clearly inclined more to unite the two than to contrast them.

As an activity that is pleasurable but that at the same time conceals the greatest values, music is ideally suited to fashion the child's play constructively. The educational process is described in some detail,[45] starting even with a prenatal procedure that consists in the application of rhythmical motion to the fetus; just as rhythm lulls infants to sleep, so will it bring about order and reason in the human being. Music of the approved sort sung to children is equally subtle and powerful. Even apart from and prior to the inculcation of ideas through sung words, musical order gains access to the soul and orders it so that in later life it will recognize reason as a friend. This is all actually a rational version of musical magic, and it is characteristic of the depth of Plato's thought that both conceptions can coexist in a single unified argument. Music produces harmony and measure in the soul, curing inner discord and immoderation; or more specifically, melody produces harmony in the soul, and rhythm measure. Music is consequently a prototype of intellectual order and truth, predisposing the later adult toward philosophy.

The child is to learn music, but to stop where the ethical values give way to a specialization that would pervert the purposes of education. This prescription has considerable support in the theories we have examined both in the *Republic* and in the *Laws*. After a certain point, indulgence in music will produce softness of character, and the acquisition of virtuosity will entail complication and distraction from more important concerns. Virtue is represented by musical simplicity, and dexterity in performance means time wasted if it is not actively pernicious in its emphasis on sensuousness. The sensuous attachment of art must be handled with extreme caution, and only as a tool in the service of virtue; yet the pleasure it provides is particularly useful in making music attractive to the child.

Doubtless the most important basis of the new conception of the *Laws* is Plato's insight into the significance of play and his incorporation of it into educational theory; *paidia* is joined to *paideia,* but not only in Plato's attention to the earlier stages of life: as it does in other transcendental works of genius created in the wise naivete of old age, play illuminates the whole life of man. Humans are the playthings of the gods, and in the happiness of peace, musical rejoicing also becomes play, like life itself. With this conception we reach the limit of musical ethics, for the aesthetic factor becomes as important as the ethical one.

III. The Philosophy and Aesthetics of Music

From what we have already discussed it is evident that theories of musical ethics are in general quite removed from the metaphysical conception of harmony, for the ethical ideas are concerned primarily with man and behavior, and almost as a corollary, with sonorous music. The distinction between the two fields of Greek musical thought can be found in the dualism of aulos and lyre which is revealed in the myths of their invention, the one by Athena and the other by Hermes.

The reed instrument was invented in imitation of human suffering, the stringed one in speculative play with a natural object—the tortoise shell—which significantly is common to both animate and inanimate nature. The one is the instrument of Dionysus, of the dithyramb, of ecstatic feeling; the other the instrument of Apollo, of the epic, of the contemplation of the world. In a musical symbol, aulos and lyre express the two fundamental attitudes of Greek musical philosophy, and if the ethical force of music comes to reside in the lyre and to disdain the aulos, this represents to some extent the entrance of the rational element of universal order into human character and emotion.

Like the metaphysics of harmony, the philosophy of ethos is based on a generalized conception of music, but the generality is of a different type: not that of the harmonic structure of nature and man, but that of the rhythmical art encompassing dance, poetry, and melody. In the philosophy of harmony, the notion of music is largely confined to pitch (rhythm makes only an occasional appearance), but sound is not retained as significant; in the ethical outlook, music is confined to sensory phenomena, but tone is joined by verbal meaning and gesture.

We reach, as a result, an extreme of concreteness, but this concreteness goes hand in hand with a lowered ontologic status, for music is here a sensory phenomenon and thus part of the deceptive world of change; even worse, it is only an imitation of other sensory phenomena, or at best a contrivance, a constructed appearance, and thus whatever power it may possess over character and behavior and feeling is accompanied by a dangerous deceptiveness: it affects us as a deceit rather than as a legitimate cause. Yet attention goes to the effect rather than the cause. That is why we cannot set out a sphere of Greek philosophy that is concerned with the imitative nature of music. Such an analysis remains subordinate to the theory of the actual moral impact of the art, which in any event has a multiplicity of causes. Ancient thought is focused on the political and educational values of sonorous music rather than on its ontology, even though music retains the metaphysical connection that is implied in the notion of imitation.

Harmony and music are accordingly quite separate in meaning, and the role of actual sound is vastly different in the two concepts. In the case of harmony, intervals and scales exist merely as the example par excellence of a conception of order to which the question of sonority is typically irrelevant; while in the case of music, whether as the concrete composite of melody and poetry and dance or as the broad sphere of the Muses (which encompasses also astronomy and forms of prose and becomes synonymous with culture as a whole), tone is present almost without exception as an essential constituent. The musical arts are certainly those of rhythm or of time; but the fact that space is subsumed in the classification by the inclusion of dance and astronomy does not mean that tone is an accidental feature. Not only is tone the most tangible embodiment of temporal rhythm, but there is very little evidence of a separate art of pure dance in Greece, while language is almost exclusively still spoken, and even astronomy is concerned with phenomena often conceived as tonal. Thus the harmony of the spheres is silent, but the music of the spheres is sonorous, which is to say that there are two sides to the Greek conception of the cosmos, just as there are two aspects of the Pythagorean outlook: scientific and poetic.

As a corollary, the Greek division of the arts was not into the categories temporal and spatial, but into temporal and static, of which the first group can equally well be called rhythmic or tonal, and there is a profound significance in the tradition that makes Mnemosyne the mother of the Muses. The distinction exists in its most distilled form in the difference between the concept of philosophy as music, which is characteristic of Socrates and the mature Plato, and the concept of dialectic as harmonic, which we find in the *Philebus.* The one points to concrete music, with its ethical effects, while the other has an abstract beauty that derives from its metaphysical background. This distinction seems to be ignored in the province of theoretical studies, where "music" is often used as a designation for "harmonics," its most characteristic representative; but to invert the figure, this is a case of *totum pro parte,* and "music" generally designates a broader type of investigation; that it can also be used as the title of a treatise on rhythmics, another of its theoretical branches, only proves the point.

But if *harmonike* is part of music, music in turn is part of *harmonia* (taking the term in its widest meaning), and this relationship holds for the sensible phenomena themselves as well as for their theory or philosophy. It is as though the temporal aspect of harmony gave rise to all the musical arts, this branch of development coming under the head of rhythm (which always tended to be an idea coordinate with harmony rather than an acclimated part of it), while the static aspect of harmony (which is connected with the pitch component of music and more faithfully transmits the meaning of the word) became increasingly identified—as harmonics—with the technical theory of music, preserving at the same time the original metaphysical significance of harmony.

More important than the distinction between the metaphysics of

harmony and the ethics of music is the fact that they are intercon-
nected; and it is their interconnection which in the last analysis is
responsible for the profundity and unity of Greek musical philosophy. Just as music is a manifestation of harmony, so the harmonic
structure of the world is informed with value; also the influence of
music rests to some extent on its harmonic order, and to this there
corresponds the ethical effect of the study of the principles of harmonics. We can go still further and say that the harmonic order of
music is responsible for the highest type of influence it is capable
of exerting, and that the ethical effect of the philosophical study of
harmony transcends the ethical effect of sonorous music.

The interconnection of the two spheres runs deeper than incidental
ramifications, as we can see if we examine Plato's musical philosophy with an eye to its overall structure. The educational influence of
music is thought of in two ways which appear to differ fundamentally but are in reality closely related. On the one hand, imitation
appears to bring about the virtue of its model, while on the other,
the harmonious and judicious application of music appears to result
in human harmony, an effect dependent upon musical order rather
than representation. But in actual fact, musical order is simply another aspect of the imitation of virtue, just as the harmony of the
tripartite soul is a fundamental aspect of virtue itself. Within the
rational part of the soul, the structure of which is discussed in the
Timaeus, harmony and order would seem to be maintained by
the corresponding features of music apart from particular imitative works or styles, but we must remember that here, too, the
order is not neutral but specifically moral, for it is that of the
diatonic genus of the Dorian mode, just as in the cosmic soul.

This is the true Greek mode, as Plato emphasizes in *Laches,*[1]
and thus has no peer in ethical value. The basic similarity of
metaphysical and ethical characteristics is especially evident in the
Timaeus, where Plato provides the links between his harmonic and
moral conceptions of music, revealing more clearly than elsewhere

that the two are not separate and that philosophy is really a unity. Since the detailed form of the world soul is that of a Dorian scale, the soul has a character which is the ideal of ethos, and thus the whole career of education will be an endeavor to approximate the true nature of cosmic structure.

Even from the outset, in the imitation of virtue, the model is more than a certain type of moral character; it is simultaneously an eternally true pattern. Of course the distinction between the sonorous imitation of virtue and the ideal force of the discipline of harmonics cannot be eliminated from Plato's outlook, and it appears to have a central place in the evolution both of his ideas and of his poetic style, turning as they do so characteristically in intellectual life from sensuous interest to abstraction.

But the *Timaeus,* still more than the *Republic* and the *Laws,* seems to make a conscious effort to unite these attitudes, not only in its picture of soul, but in an analysis of the mechanism of the effect of sonorous music, which is really a problem that concerns the relationship of ethos and harmony, and that consequently is crucial with respect to the unity of Plato's musical conceptions. The higher ethical ideal of rational order is explicitly depicted as the outcome of actual music, and at the same time—if we can apply the concept of imitation in this regard—music is imitative of the structure of reality rather than of the actions of man. This is an imitation that turns more or less directly to the Ideas for its model, skipping over the phenomenal world much more decidedly than any kind of ideal imitation based on the activity of the imagination, which simply selects and combines the desirable features of a multiplicity of physical objects, introducing at most a distortion or modification of the factual so as to produce a more convincing impression. Rhythm is part of the picture, but the whole notion concerns a musical action that is prior to and apart from any content presented by words and also without reliance on or relation to the particular characteristics of individual works of art.

However impressive this conception may be, its strength is not aesthetic in the sense of a concentration on perceptible properties, but lies rather in its splendid breadth of vision. But the aesthetic implications are there, and indeed they are peculiarly characteristic of the Greek interest in ideal forms, for what the *Timaeus* holds up is the pattern for all of music, a pattern that is to underlie the particularities of every work of value and to count as the chief source of its beauty. The controlling notion is no longer that of materialistically conceived imitation, but one of an intrinsic musical order—more proper to instrumental music—which is comparable to the science of harmonics in its moral influence.

In this view, music produces inside us a human imitation of divine harmony, so that the conception treats of nothing less than an interaction of what the future was to know as *musica instrumentalis, humana* and *mundana.* The ethical task of music consists in bringing the music of man into accord with its cosmic prototype. In open contradiction to Plato's notoriously negative evaluation of art, music takes on not only a superior ethical worth but a high status also in respect of truth and knowledge. Even the aesthetic values of beauty and pleasure appear in an unexpectedly favorable light, for they partake of reason as well as sense.

The mutual relations of music and harmony in respect of ethics can be seen to excellent advantage in Greek education, which we can actually characterize in general as the study of music; indeed the various departments of study all appear to grow out of music, lower education from musical practice and higher from musical theory. Liberal education was not a process of imparting knowledge but of fashioning and cultivating the character; as an ethical undertaking it revolved initially around practical music. The older of the two aspects of *paideia* was centered on the leisured musical pursuits of an aristocracy to which was added the civic ceremonial of the polis; preparation for participation in symposium and choral dance was thus the basic motivation.

To this original concept of musical cultivation, which already had become evident in the Homeric world, the Pythagoreans added the speculative interest in mathematics, again musical in nature, but concerned with theoretical or harmonic matters rather than with composition and performance. The interest was now not purely moral, but was divided between metaphysics and ethics, while the ethical values were no longer of a concrete social nature but rather of a transcendent personal aspiration that was both religious and philosophical. That harmonics was diffused throughout the Pythagorean *mathemata,* we have already seen, and thus it is possible to consider these studies as essentially equivalent to musical theory, provided we keep in mind that the larger philosophical significance of harmony was a fundamental part of their scope. But the older concern with sonorous music was also in effect a group of subjects rather than one, for musical composition and performance meant ability in dance, song, and lyre playing. Although they were connected with dance, gymnastics stood somewhat apart because of their connection with military prowess and later increasingly with athletics and sport. Grammar was more completely a part of the musical complex, which consequently can be thought of as dealing with a linguistic composite of meaning, melody, and rhythm, plus the additional manifestation of rhythm in dance. Clearly the traditional compact description of the lower education as music and gymnastics was an accurate representation of its contents.

But it was also conceived of as an *enkyklios paideia,*[2] a cultivation that would seem to pertain to the *kyklios,* or circle, of the choral dance, although the meaning of the term may have been reinforced by the coincidence that the scolion, too, involved a circle as the singing passed around the table to each guest in turn. Thus the *enkyklios paideia* had an aristocratic and specifically ethical connotation, designating education for a cultivated and urbane way of life and in particular for the chief manifestation of this life in music; although the concept is old, the word was apparently not formulated until the time of Plato. It is only such an origin, however, that is capable of explaining the peculiar selection of subjects that constituted a liberal education. With the decline of these musical institutions and their society, philosophy and rhetoric fought over the right of succession.

We can see in Plato's *Theaetetus* in particular how the whole musical conception with its class prerogative of leisure and its scorn for the servitude of practical occupations is taken over by philosophy.[3] Rhetoric becomes the antithesis, representing illiberal employment for gain. A specific terminology based on music contrasts the two classes, and this is also adopted by philosophy. Conscious of its role as a successor of music, philosophy even invades the symposium and supplants song, and the Platonic Academy similarly replaces the music of the poetic school with discussion.

But in terms of educational trends and the whole temper of society, it is rhetoric that conquers; grammar becomes a separate subject of increasing importance, and eventually the *enkyklios paideia* is transformed into the trivium of the encyclical studies, rhetoric and logic joining grammar in the service of oratory. Gymnastics and music, almost invisible, make a modest contribution to the same end, and even the quadrivial studies are drawn into service. This process begins during the course of the fifth century B.C.; the disintegration of the composite art of music, accompanied by political ferment and the growth of a rhetorically minded culture, brings about the demusicalization of education. With these changes, the *enkyklios paideia* begins to expand its scope, and the term itself is used in a more general and preparatory sense, as we can find it in Aristotle, to mean usual or customary; the ethical significance also fades.

Even in the time of Socrates, rhetoric had already laid claim to the mathematical studies, and during the Hellenistic era these came to be included in the concept of encyclical education. At the same time, the Roman interpretation of *enkyklios paideia* as a "circle," or group, of studies (*orbis doctrinae*) left the limited and specific selection of the subjects unaccounted for; new ethical aims could easily be set for the whole, and the most prominent of these was supplied by the theological outlook of late antiquity and the Middle Ages. Finally the term became "encyclopedia"; the "circle" was widened to the universality of encyclopedic knowledge as conceived in modern times. That the concept and the term absorbed the *mathemata* and not vice versa, and indeed eventually absorbed all of knowledge, confirms the essentially ethical nature of sonorous music and education. Science extended and deepened the ethical goals by adding new ones, but neither science nor education as a whole was ever concerned in antiquity with knowledge for its own sake, which, like art for its own sake, is an exceptional concept of recent times and hardly ever found in undiluted form.

If the departments of the *enkyklios paideia,* like those of the *mathemata,* are tied together by musical factors, it is not surprising that the same bond unites the two divisions in their entirety. But can the higher education be considered literally as the theory of the lower? If so, the Greek concept of the identity of doing and knowing would find confirmation, and education as a whole would have the strongest possible unity, even if that unity—as Plato believed— could be fully realized only by a few superior people.

Now the theoretical study of the subjects of the *enkyklios paideia* can be fairly accurately represented by harmonics and rhythmics, taking harmonics to apply to melody and rhythmics to apply to both poetry and dance. Thus rhythmics would comprise metrics and orchestics, if these existed as separate disciplines. The fact that words rather than gesture were later used as a basis for the study of rhythmics does not upset the correspondence, for the preference may not have existed in classical times, and in any event, the particular manifestation used is of no real importance, since rhythmical theory has a perfectly general applicability to motion and temporal phenomena. To harmonics and rhythmics we can add the theory of grammar, which was doubtless later than the others to develop.

But harmonics, rhythmics, and grammar are not the sciences constituting the *mathemata,* which apparently have a different source and grow from harmony rather than practical music, so that they have from the start a metaphysical and cosmological interest. Other musical disciplines may have existed also, such as those bearing on composition and performance and even on the function and utility of music. Practical studies of the theory of composition and performance would doubtless remain tied to practice even if they were formalized, while theories of the ethical value of music belong neither in lower nor higher education but above them both, in philosophy, although for details in this field Plato turns to Damon, that is, to the sphere of professional education.

But it must be admitted that we do not know the status of the basic disciplines of harmonics, rhythmics, and grammar; we can only guess that the rudiments of these subjects were taken up as part of the *enkyklios paideia,* and that they received full and adequate treatment in the field of professional or technical training. In addition, harmonics, and rhythmics as part of it, was represented in the *mathemata.* The equivocal position of these various subjects, which continues into the later history of education, is of particular interest in pointing to the existence of various types of theory, differing in degree of practicality.

Most conspicuously, harmonics has a dual relationship: it is the theory of melos but it is also part of the *mathemata.* Thus there may very well have been two harmonic disciplines, one more practical in orientation and one more speculative; it is too much to expect these interests to coincide, so that the details of musical structure, for example, will be of purely theoretic value in mathematics or philosophy; the theories of Plato undoubtedly represent a remarkable rapprochement in this respect. In any event, it has become apparent that the larger relationship between practical and theoretical education cannot be described as a simple correspondence.

If theoretical studies can originate through the reflective examina-

Philosophy and Aesthetics of Music   97

tion of practice, it is equally the case that practical subjects can arise
through the application of theory. This furnishes a new light in
which to inspect the _enkyklios paideia_. Music, or at any rate melody,
is certainly the practical manifestation of harmonic theory; but the
other disciplines of the _mathemata_ had their applied forms also,
although the presence of these in lower education is justified more
by everyday utility and a truly primary educational function.

The best established of them was logistic, or calculation, which
was the study of applied arithmetic. This was usually taught in
connection with letters, or elementary grammar, a practice that
shows where the true emphasis was placed; pupils were asked, for
example, to tell the number of letters in a word. But calculation was
also taught in a variety of concrete illustrations and in connection
with a number of games, so as to make it a pleasurable activity.
Geodesy, or mensuration, which was applied geometry, was a part
of lower education too, and involved simple problems in the measurement of length, area, and volume; while astronomy was represented by the study of the calendar. These were all later additions
to the curriculum, however; we find Plato still urging their importance.

In Platonic thought, the matter of applied and pure mathematics
is highly significant ethically, for it arises in connection with a
conception of mathematics as leading from the material to the ideal;
but Aristotle is no less concerned with the problem, for in a somewhat similar way, he places mathematics between physical science
and philosophy, and deals systematically with its relationship to
these two areas.[4] Thus he gives formal recognition to a series of
applied mathematical sciences and at the same time reveals more of
the complexity of the whole question, transplanting it essentially
from ethics to metaphysics. Harmonics, optics, mechanics, and phenomena (observational astronomy) become the more physical departments of mathematics, presupposing respectively arithmetic, geometry, geometry and stereometry, and spherics (theoretical astron-

omy). Even without considering here the detailed features of this conception of physical mathematics, we can see that these studies are hardly the concrete examples of applied mathematics that had a place in lower education. On the other hand harmonics is carefully distinguished from the abstract theory of proportion, which becomes part of arithmetic and is made use of in harmonics only in conjunction with the facts of physical acoustics and auditory perception, and only to the extent that it corresponds to these facts. The study of proportion as a purely theoretical type of harmonics not specifically related to music may have existed nowhere but in Plato's imagination.

If harmonics exists as a discipline derived from music and also as a branch of the *mathemata* or a division of physical mathematics, another ambivalence can be found in the case of astronomy, which is one of the Muses as well as one of the *mathemata*. In Aristotle's scheme it is also a branch of physical mathematics, and we have seen that it had an applied form in lower education, but our present concern is that it belongs to the conception of music contained in the developed classical system of the nine Muses. This comprised the various forms of *mousike,* including epic and lyric poetry, drama, history, dance, and astronomy.

Evidently the classification represents a sophisticated point of view in which the original *mousike* has been elaborated and in part dissected into component arts. The presence of astronomy can be explained in general by the mathematical and synesthetic connections between the cosmos and music, but the particular explanation for its presence where the other members of the *mathemata* are absent is that it deals with motion even more essentially than harmonics does, while arithmetic and geometry are concerned with static entities. Astronomy can become a Muse, which is to say it can become sonorous, because motion connects it with sonority; just as harmony—not harmonics—can be the mother of the Muses because its broad domain comprises temporal manifestations as well as static. Thus the interconnection of art and science that is revealed in the sphere of education with respect to ethical influences can also be found in the general province of the Muses, and it becomes increasingly clear why culture in general was conceived as musical.

The universality of harmonic thought can be seen again in the interrelation of the theoretical studies we have derived from the *enkyklios paideia:* harmonics, rhythmics, and grammar. In its power to classify and to reduce the infinite to order, formal analysis is conceived by Plato as the very foundation of knowledge. The conception is doubtless an extension of Pythagorean ideas, and the model of the procedure—as we have mentioned in Chapter One—is provided by harmonics.

In the *Cratylus*,[5] where language is conceived as an imitation comparable in general to music and painting, Socrates undertakes an analysis of grammar that presumably would have its parallel in harmonics and geometry. But actually he uses rhythmics as a parallel; the simple and compound durations with which this discipline is concerned are comparable to the various letter sounds and the syllables of grammar. Behind rhythmics, however, there stands proportional theory and thus harmonics.

The discussion in the *Philebus*[6] is even more interesting. Plato takes rhythmics and harmonics as parallels to grammar, and rhythmics is related to bodily motion rather than to words; thus there is a strong suggestion of a basic division of music into gesture, melody, and meaning. The comparison between grammar and harmonics is especially close: "The sound which passes through the lips whether of an individual or of all men is one and yet infinite. And yet not by knowing either that sound is one or that sound is infinite are we perfect in the art of speech, but the knowledge of the number and nature of sounds is what makes a man a grammarian. And the knowledge which makes a man a musician is of the same kind." He goes on to separate sounds in respect of pitch into high, low, and middle, and then in the grammatical analysis shortly afterwards, separates them analogously into vowels, semivowels, and mutes. The detailed analysis of melody and rhythm shows how intimately related the theories of harmonics and rhythmics are to musical practice:

But when you have learned what sounds are high and what low, and the number and nature of the intervals and their limits or proportions, and the systems compounded out of them, which our fathers discovered, and have handed down to us who are their descendants under the name of harmonies; and the affections corresponding to them in the movements of the human body, which when measured by numbers ought, as they say, to be called rhythms and measures; and they tell us that the same principle should be applied to every one and many;—when, I say, you have learned all this, then, my dear friend, you are perfect; and you may be said to understand any other subject, when you have a similar grasp of it. But the infinity of kinds and the infinity of individuals which there is in each of them, when not classified, creates in every one of us a state of infinite ignorance; and he who never looks for number in anything, will not himself be looked for in the number of famous men.

A Pythagorean origin is indicated by the numerical basis of this analysis, and this strengthens the general feeling that the congruence of all three fields—harmonics, rhythmics, and grammar—is due to the fact that they are all theoretical abstractions from an original verbal-musical unity. And we are once again reminded of the Pythagorean faith in number by the discussion of knowledge in the *Theaetetus,* where the method of division is also illustrated by grammar; this time, however, grammar is used in conjunction with arithmetic, and letters are expressly coupled with the elements of all things.[7] With harmonics, then, arithmetic also enters into the grammatical as well as the rhythmical department of the *enkyklios paideia.*

As the discussions in Plato make clear, the letters, syllables, words, and articulate speech of grammar correspond to the tones, intervals, systems, and melody of harmonics, and also to the durations, feet, meters, and poetic form of rhythmics. But this correspondence, as we have indicated, is not simply the result of the same system of analysis applied to three different fields; the relationship is much closer and has its explanation in the fact that all three disciplines arose from the unity of actual music. The element of grammar seems to have been not the *gramma,* or letter, but the *stoicheion,*[8] a sonorous entity, a vowel sound; speech and melody both involved the organization of tone, one according to verbal reason and the other according to pitch. Rhythm was the organization of durational form, and also followed harmonic principles. The identity of vowel sound and tone is clearly shown by solmization; the vowel was the only way to realize the vocal tone, but still more, it revealed the serial position of the tone in the tetrachord, and was thus directly coordinated with pitch.

Thus the grammatical *stoicheia* were measured tones capable of serial arrangement, and not simply elemental constituents indifferent in nature. This new concept of element can have originated only in music, although it soon developed into a general word for elements of any type. If in their search for first principles the Pythagoreans turned from the notion of primitive material constituents to formal ones, if they found their archai, as Aristotle reports, in number, then the concept of *stoicheion* can with some probability be attributed to them, especially since such a serial constituent was both numerical and harmonic and could very well have been durational also. The numbers they found in all things could here have been concrete tones of defined pitch and duration, possibly thought of in addition as the bearers of conceptual meaning. Again it is in the fifth century, shortly after the term *stoicheion* itself appears, that the *stoicheion* of grammar begins to change into the *gramma;* the sonorous and tonal "element" becomes identified with its symbol, a visual and purely linguistic "letter." But the connection of grammar and harmonics persists as a parallel for centuries.

If the penetration of the *enkyklios paideia* by quantitative thought is one of the epochal innovations of the Pythagoreans, then their acoustical discoveries in which the analysis of tone led them to cosmic theories were only one of the aspects of their achievement. A corresponding analysis of the other phases of music yields rhythmics and grammar, which like harmonics, represent the rationalization of music according to the principles of number.

As we have seen, these principles are responsible for the theoretical treatment of the *enkyklios paideia,* adding applied science to musical practice and thus directly abetting musical-verbal skill. The same principles applied to the external world and to being in general produce the *mathemata.* In these two procedures we have the direct causes of two different disciplines of harmonics. This study will have a practical orientation if it is derived from melodic experience, while if it insists upon a rational basis derived from the speculative harmonics of the *mathemata,* which is really grounded in the proportional theory of arithmetic, it will have a theoretic orientation. Musical harmonics of this sort came to be known as canonics, because it was based on the canon, the rule or measured scale applied to the monochord.

There is really no end to the physical models that can be found for mathematics, and thus the number of practical applications of the branches of the *mathemata* is indefinitely large. Musical harmonics and music itself are only two of many exemplifications of speculative harmonics, and drawing, which Aristotle mentions in the *Politics* as part of lower education, is equally with the very different study of geodesy or of geography, an instance of applied geometry; drawing and painting, as a matter of fact, are quite like music in status, while a good counterpart of canonics would be optics, and the analogue of practical harmonics would be mechanics. But in addition to the complex array of applied mathematical sciences there are also mystic pseudo-sciences that parallel the disciplines of the *mathemata,* although they do not come into prominence until Neo-Pythagorean times. Numerology, astrology, and a mystical variety of harmonics are of considerable importance; they actually descend from the older universal sphere of harmonic thought that found itself in large measure unrepresented in the new specialization and definition of sciences. This consideration helps to explain the wide variety of subject matter found in the harmonic treatises of late antiquity.

From an ethical point of view, the connection between lower and higher education finds its finest expression in Plato's Seventh Letter; philosophy cannot simply be imparted but must be lived. Similarly music predisposes the soul for reason; the lower education has a completely distinct mode of action from the higher, magically preforming the soul; in some cases the educational process can go no further. In general, however, the relationship between the lower and higher educations can be clarified by the consideration that just as theory has its manifestations in practice, so conduct and behavior as well as formative activity can be reflected upon and thus develop their own theory. Both processes are effective, although the emphasis may lie on one or the other at different times.

Thus a productive and ethical interest constitutes the chief feature of music, and to this a specific brand of theory is relevant as a guide or an explanation; while an originally speculative interest in the natural world, on the other hand, can find a practical exemplification in music, and in this situation both domains can be mutually suggestive. In ancient Greece, these two interests were of coordinate importance and of reciprocal influence, although they are manifested at different times and in different kinds of writings; in the Middle Ages, by contrast, the scientific or speculative interest predominates, whether allied to theology or in isolation; while in modern times, practice with its special theory and its history is in the foreground. As far as sonorous music is concerned, the theoretic attitude emphasizes the musical system as a whole, and the practical one individual works of art as personal and cultural expressions, along with the analytic laws that can be derived from them. Modern conceptions are clearly more concerned with aesthetic properties per se.

The Hellenic conception of music, then, can be thought of as constituted by the intersection of two points of view, the metaphysical and the aesthetic-ethical, and the relative contributions of the two factors are determined by the overall philosophic outlook. Heraclitus' words, the hidden harmony is better than the visible one, can be taken to express the antisensuous tendency of harmony; while in terms of the Platonic conception of Ideas, the highest value will reside in a harmony that transcends the material world altogether. In such a setting, ideas of harmony in art become strangely equivocal with respect to aesthetic value. That sense will give way to reason follows almost as a corollary from Plato's abstract concept of beauty, which paradoxically is itself expressed by Socrates with great emotional power and sensuous beauty in the *Phaedrus* and the *Symposium*. Here the artist and the philosopher in Plato are at odds, and they meet only in the more severe beauty of the later dialogues.

As concrete species of harmony, all the sensible arts must manifest the abstract features of harmonic order, almost in spite of their perceptible nature. There was no difficulty about applying notions of harmony to visual art; in the middle of the fifth century B.C., Empedocles already describes the painter's mixture of pigments as a harmony. Plato's discussions of harmony in art are often completely general. In the *Statesman*,[9] for example, the highest class of the good—which the *Philebus* determines to be that of measure and the mean—is revealed as the foundation of art. The very existence of the arts depends on the possibility of measuring more or less, and of measuring them not only with respect to one another but also with a view to attaining the mean; while the excellence or beauty of every work of art is due to the observance of measure.

Thus in its application to art, the conception of harmony can give rise to aesthetic value; the superior beauty of rational harmony comes to reside in a sensible work, and provides the ultimate basis of perceived beauty. This has a counterpart in the inherence of absolute beauty in the physical beauty of a human being, which is described in one of the most moving passages of the *Phaedrus*.

The same aesthetic is applied to music in the *Philebus:* "And whereas the high and low, the swift and the slow are infinite or unlimited, does not the addition of the principles aforesaid introduce a limit, and perfect the whole frame of music?" [10] Since the discussion is designed to illustrate the harmonic division of existence into classes, music is understandably so apt an illustration that it has the force of the general conception as well as of a particular instance. The *Philebus* not only identifies metaphysics with aesthetics, however, but regards the highest ethical values also—measure and the mean and symmetry—as aesthetic in effect and beautiful in nature. Even the element of pleasure is present, for the mixture of the finite and infinite yields not only the beauties of body and soul, but all the delights of life.

If the *Philebus* is concerned with the inherently harmonic nature of metaphysics and ethics and thus with their beauty, the *Gorgias* [11] points to the ethical implications of harmony in art. All artists dispose things in order and compel one part to harmonize and accord with the other parts; but when the artist's activity affects man in substantial degree, it will obviously lose its purely aesthetic character. The trainer and physician give harmony and order to the body, where they have the effect of health and strength; and similarly, the true rhetorician and the man who is morally good give harmony and order to the soul, where their effect is temperance and justice, or in a word, virtue. Thus we arrive again in the familiar territory of the ethical nature of harmony.

But art often suffers by comparison with the precise qualities of abstract harmony. In the *Philebus,* for example, music appears as the paragon of dialectic method, as the science of tone; and during the division of pleasure and wisdom into their species, it is placed, quite consistently, not among the pleasures, but among the sciences and arts, the classes of wisdom and knowledge. But this context is its undoing, for it is assigned to the impure variety of the productive or handicraft class of knowledge (which is opposed to the educational class). As compared with carpentry, for example, music is less exact in its results and full of empiricism. "Sounds are harmonized not by measure but by skillful conjecture; the music of the aulos is always trying to guess the pitch of each vibrating note and is therefore mixed up with much that is doubtful, and has little which is certain." [12]

But this view of music, which reveals the generality of the Greek conception of art and makes music essentially the same in nature as science and craft, is more or less restricted to instrumental performance; it is the aulos player or the lyre player who is found in the company of scribes, pilots, and weavers. Imitation plays no part in the conception; the knowledge involved is in no way suspect or second-rate. When the notion of imitation enters, all this is radically altered. Music is separated from the sciences and the crafts, harmony and the aesthetic values connected with it are overlooked; instead music takes on ethical properties and is subjected to standards of truth and morality. The object of imitation is the determinant of artistic character. Instrumental music becomes deficient in clarity. If the object of imitation is insufficiently known by the artist, as is typical in rhetoric, the art traffics in appearance only and becomes flattery instead of art; this is Plato's view of sophistry, rhetoric, cooking, and the art of clothing the body, as opposed to the arts of legislation, justice, gymnastics, and medicine, which are based on knowledge.

To some extent, philosophy is open to the same objection (especially in the dramatic form of the dialogue), for discourse too, as we read in the *Critias,* is only an imitation.[13] The same dialogue illustrates the identification of philosophy and music, on which we have placed so much emphasis; even the traditional musical *topos* of praise is represented in both. Before Critias begins his discourse, Hermocrates says: "First invoke Apollo and the Muses, and then let us hear you sound the praises and show forth the virtues of your ancient citizens." [14] Generally, though, a higher value is placed on philosophy, in contrast with the other imitative arts. Socrates says in the *Eryxias,* for example, "My argument, Critias, appears to have given you the same kind of pleasure which you might have derived from some rhapsode's recitation of Homer, for you do not believe a word of what has been said." [15]

The essential difference between the two basic conceptions of art is that in the one case—that of instrumental music—the knowledge of the artist is a knowledge of the intrinsic properties of his art, while in the other, it is a knowledge, demonstrably second-hand, of external matters which are incorporated in the work of art and become its "content." Instrumental music will not easily permit such treatment, however, and insists on the values of the artistic process itself, achieving at least the dignity of craft if not of science.

Yet the highest worth is denied to it unless it becomes transparent and thus in some fashion imitative; as an opaque transaction dealing with physical material it remains bound to the world of sense and appearance. In every instance value lies in seeing through sense; this overcomes both the inexactness and the indirectness of the image, for we are led to contemplate the suprasensuous reality in which it participates. Thus music of any type assumes an ethical function: instrumental music reveals the harmonic Forms, and imitative music, by turning to objects that are good and by truly knowing and representing them, ultimately conducts us through them to the same end. Beauty is never purely sensuous pleasure, but will depend on the rational element of order; it is greatest when the order is metaphysically and ethically most significant, and declines when structural complexity goes beyond the pattern of nature. Thus an isolated tone has a small degree of beauty, while the complex "panharmonic" style is not beautiful at all.

Evidently beauty and truth and goodness are covariant, and beauty is little more than the appeal of being to sense, or preferably the appeal of being to reason. It is the soul's recognition of its counterpart in the order of nature. Thus beauty is related to love, for it summons up the desire of love, and in this way it becomes known.

But love, although it is awakened by sensuous beauty, has its true object in the Idea of beauty, which is the original home of the soul. And in the soul's remembrance of this home lies the explanation of our love of beauty as well as of the nature of this love, which impels us into transcendental regions. Eros, accordingly, is half human and half divine; it is philosophic love; and beauty cannot be fully realized by the physical world, especially not by art, but only by the love of the soul in conjunction with philosophy. The center of gravity in Plato's aesthetics lies outside the physical work of art, but unless the role of sense is removed altogether, we cannot say that aesthetic value is neglected; it is only physical beauty as such for which Plato has little respect, not physical beauty in conjunction with ideal factors. The *Symposium* clearly characterizes the two constituents of music, noetic and sensible, overlooking completely the more obvious contrast of material model and musical image:

Again, in the essential nature of harmony and rhythm there is no difficulty in discerning love which has not yet become double. But when you want to use them in actual life, either in the composition of songs or in the correct performance of airs or metres composed already, which latter is called education, then the difficulty begins, and the good artist is needed. Then the old tale has to be repeated of fair and heavenly love—the love of Urania the fair and heavenly Muse, and of the duty of accepting the temperate, and those who are as yet intemperate only that they may become temperate, and of preserving their love; and again, of the vulgar Polyhymnia, who must be used with circumspection that the pleasure be enjoyed, but may not generate licentiousness.[16]

Aesthetics and education appear together, and with them appear pleasure and all the dangers of imitation.

In a dualistic system of appearance and ideal forms, then, music will become a sensuous manifestation of reason. The sensible and changing *harmoniai* with their multiplicity of genera, all produced by particular tensions of strings and of the voice, are the approximate realization of underlying *systemata* and ideal ratios.[17] Meters and rhythms also are the perceptible expression of changeless harmonic proportions. Conceived in the *Timaeus* as a work of art, the world contained an imperceptible harmonic logos that music incorporated with peculiar adequacy. The words of articulate song were another imitation close to the inherent nature of both physical and ideal entities; these were the human side of the musical composite, although language too was divine in its origin and represented divinity in man. Music, spontaneous and demonic, was penetrated by both the cosmic and the human aspects of reason. Orpheus and Pythagoras had caused it to comprise both language and mathematics; after the classical age these were separated out, leaving again, at least for a time, only pleasure in sound.

When the ideal forms became aesthetic, however, they made perceptible not only metaphysical truth but also beauty and virtue. The beauty had a transcendental tendency; if it did not point to a higher nonaesthetic beauty, it had to retain a connection with some sensible manifestation of virtue, which it did by imitation, for solely as nonimitative pleasure in sensation it was no more than beauty of an elementary type. Thus as soon as music became perceptible it became ethical, but it did so—if we except the contribution of the verbal constituent—through its rhythm rather than its harmony. The connection with the human soul—with feelings as well as character—was through motion, made palpable in dance but not found in pitch until it became temporal succession or rhythm. The abstract relationships of harmonics were the timeless Ideas prior to life, and only in the clothing of duration, of tone and word and rhythm, did they have an immediate relation to the motions of the human body and soul.

It was accordingly the aesthetic side of music that introduced the particularities of imitation, the qualities of character found in all the varieties of linguistic, ethnological, and personal constitution; these were manifested in language dialects, dances, meters, modes, intruments, and tempo. But this diversity was brought into a systematic order based on typical Hellenic characteristics, notably those expressed in the lyre and in the Dorian mode; and since this particular character was the most virtuous and beautiful and intelligent of all, the musical system it developed possessed attributes that went beyond those of a particular imitation to incorporate ideal forms, and its transparent aesthetic surface revealed truth, beauty, and goodness in themselves.

To Plato's eyes the revelation of truth through sense appeared as a miracle. Concepts could be formulated by generalization based on individual instances, and art could similarly enhance its value by refining away particularities. But the participation of sensible entities in the Ideas provided no easy access to the supernal world; only a lifelong labor of love, a slow and painstaking ascent of the rungs of sense, opinion, and understanding would permit us to step across to reason and truth, which have a completely different nature. The artist, however, does not proceed by this human route, nor does he grasp truth directly by reason; he knows it and captures it in tangible form by a divine madness; his inspiration and its source are attested to by the fact that he cannot account for what he creates.[18]

IV. The Peripatetics

Even during the fifth century B.C., the Pythagorean and Platonic conception of music was subjected to serious criticism; polemics and alternative ideas were a prelude to the better documented controversy and to the whole expansion and modification of the classical outlook that were brought about by Peripatetic philosophy. We can only speculate about the circumstances of Damon's banishment, although we cannot escape the suggestion that his musical theories may have been vigorously contested; but there is no doubt that the conflict during Plato's lifetime between the old education and the new, and between rhetoric and philosophy, involved fundamental notions of the nature and influence of music.

Certainly the social and ethical role of music was called into question by the psychologism and individualism of Euripides and by the intellectual relativism and skepticism of the Sophists; the *Frogs* and the *Clouds* of Aristophanes leave no room for doubt on this score. Whether through individualism or relativism, the currents that spelled the end of the civilization of the polis concerned themselves with the musical expression and manipulation of feelings if not solely with musical pleasure; the more lasting effects of music on the character, which are the heart of its social function, were disregarded and probably disbelieved, an attitude that would inevitably have had its corollary in metaphysical and harmonic ideas also. In the total range of musical aesthetics, feelings occupy a position between moral values and purely aesthetic characteristics such as beauty and pleasure; a psychological and rhetorical motivation will thus entail an abandonment of the social conception of music in favor of a greater interest in perceptual properties for their own sake.

It is not easy to determine just how music was involved in the disagreement between the Sophists and Socrates or in the later

differences between Isocrates and Plato. Musical study was certainly
of recognized value in rhetorical education; the early Sophists endorsed it in both practical and theoretical form, although it obviously does not follow that their reasons for doing so were the same
as those of Plato or that their conception of its nature and effects
was compatible with his.

In Plato's *Menexenus*,[1] Socrates speaks very highly of Aspasia, his
teacher in rhetoric, and tells Menexenus that "besides her I had
Connus, the son of Metrobius, as a master, and he was my master in
music, as she was in rhetoric. No wonder that a man who has
received such an education should be a finished speaker; even the
pupil of very inferior masters, say, for example, one who had learned
music of Lamprus, and rhetoric of Antiphon the Rhamnusian,
might make a figure if he were to praise the Athenians among the
Athenians."

Still more significantly, the true rhetoric of the *Phaedrus* is fully
compatible with philosophy and its musical nature. Rhetoric was a
logical extension of the study of letters and at first simply an expansion of lower education as it began to assume the purely literary
character it manifests in late antiquity. But if Socrates was in agreement with the educational views of the Sophists in some respects, he
also had broader notions of the value of music that went well beyond its utility to the orator, and with these the Sophists would
logically have been in serious disagreement.

An outspokenly skeptical view of the ethical and expressive powers of music is found in a fragment of an oration delivered at Hibeh
in Egypt by an Athenian speaker, probably in the time of Plato.[2]
The orator undertakes to refute the notion that "some melodies
make us equable, others reasonable, others righteous, others brave,
and others cowardly," by citing as fact that the people living in the
area of the Thermopylae, whose music is diatonic, are braver than
the tragedians, who sing enharmonic melodies exclusively, although
this genus purportedly produces courage. Similarly, he asserts, chro-

matic music does not create fearfulness. Adopting a rhetorical tone, he goes on to attack the qualifications of those who uphold the notion of musical influences. They are specialists in nothing, certainly not in music or argumentation, but this does not stop them from playing and singing in a ridiculously poor fashion or from asserting "that certain melodies are related to the laurel tree and others to the ivy plant." Reference to the symbols of Apollo and Dionysus serves here to satirize the description of melodies as ethical and orgiastic. The oration expresses the scientific attitude of the musical specialist, and it is apparently directed against the philosopher. Especially interesting is the slur cast on the rhetorical ability of the upholders of ethos, for it indicates that the target was in all probability Socrates and Plato, the chief critics of rhetoric.

At the same time, the Sophists—skilled in rhetoric and convinced that truth was relative to the observer—explicitly denied the objectivity of values, and as the arch-opponents of the two philosophers, would logically have urged complete skepticism with respect to the ethical and social force of music; in Plato's view they were unmusical technicians, and thus not even capable of understanding Socrates' intense devotion to music and Plato's insistence upon its importance. It is possible also, of course, that the Hibeh oration was directed specifically against Damon's *Areopagiticus;* in any event the polemic attacks precisely the social philosopher of musical ethics, who subscribed to the various but constant moral and emotional effects of music, and not the Pythagoreans, who believed in the moderating, purifying, and ordering force of harmony. If the speech is directed against Damon it is certainly in error in representing him as a musical dilettante, while Plato, who fused the views of Damon with those of Pythagoras, and Aristotle also, might be charged correctly with being musical amateurs; indeed they both take pains to point out their lack of technical knowledge.

Before the Peripatetics, only the Sophists have left appreciable evidence of musical views differing from those of the Pythagoreans and Plato. Yet musical practice was dominated by a hedonist aesthetic which was combatted with vigor by both Plato and Aristophanes. From their arguments it is clear that they were vitally interested in confuting the thesis that music represents pleasure rather than virtue and individual feelings rather than traditional moral values. The existence of such a thesis is unmistakably implied by the music of the period, which was characterized repeatedly as lascivious and virtuosic, but the explicit philosophic statement that would endorse an art of this kind has disappeared without a trace. Nor can we impute a belief in the immorality of music to proponents of hedonism like the Cyrenaics, for pleasure need not conflict with ethical value; Plato regards pleasure as an important and useful accompanying charm of music, while in Aristotle's philosophy it exists side by side with moral aims as a coordinate musical effect.

By the same token, ethical skepticism such as that expressed in the Hibeh oration is not necessarily accompanied by a positive conception of music as purely a source of pleasure or an expression of joy or as no more than a stimulus or expression of feelings. Thus one can find music inherently pleasurable but also ethical, or in no way ethical but not, as a result, pleasurable or expressive. The social disdain and ascetic ideals of the Cynics have more direct consequences for musical ethics, and indeed Diogenes Laertius informs us that Diogenes of Sinope, the notorious student of Antisthenes, looked upon music as useless;[3] musicians who were able to tune the lyre did not give similar attention to the moral attributes of the soul.

The musical views of the atomist Democritus,[4] probably the greatest contemporary of Socrates, are difficult to determine; in all likelihood they were not very different from Pythagorean and Platonic conceptions. Enjoyment and happiness (eudaemonia) based on moderation of pleasure and on pleasure in beauty is well provided by music, but there is every reason to feel that this type of pleasure is a natural partner and not an opponent of virtue, and that Democritus is equally favorable to both. Sensory qualities may exist

merely by convention, but their distance from metaphysical truth is
no incontrovertible argument against their moral influence, just as it
is no argument against their beauty or pleasantness. And similarly,
that music is the youngest of the arts, that it was not created by
necessity but arose from superfluity, does not mean that it is morally
impotent. It can only be urged that in default of a metaphysical
theory of harmony, those moral effects could not be present that
depend upon the structural identity of music with the soul and the
cosmos; but the influences dependent upon representation would be
relatively unaffected. As a matter of fact, Democritus evidently gave
considerable attention to music, writing on rhythm and harmony,
on poetry, and on the beauty of words and the euphony of letters.
Unfortunately these must be placed among the numberless ancient
treatises on music that have been lost.

Aristoxenus, the renowned pupil of Aristotle, accompanies a re-
mark about the effect of music on the character with the qualifica-
tion "in so far as musical art can improve the moral character."[5]
But this reservation is an exception; the Peripatetics did not question the ethical significance of music, although they modified the
inherited conception in important ways. On the other hand, Aristotle's skepticism with regard to the metaphysical significance of
harmony is quite striking, for it constitutes a vital part of his labori-
ous and detailed rejection of Platonic idealism. One of the outcomes
of this rejection is that music is evicted from ontology, although, as
we shall see presently, the eviction appears to entail an increased
interest in music as a sonorous phenomenon, in the physical and
psychological properties of tone. Peripatetic philosophy becomes
concerned with musical questions that are technical, scientific, and
empirical, and that by way of this route also occasionally deal with
specifically aesthetic matters. In general, Aristotle's views would appear to resemble those of Democritus; Proclus tells us that they both
believed names to arise by chance rather than by nature; and in both
philosophers the fact that harmony and number are deprived of

independent reality would logically weaken the theory of the ethical nature of music and tend to focus attention on sensuous enjoyment.

The basis of Aristotle's attitude towards harmony is best seen in the *Metaphysics,*[6] which makes quite explicit his disbelief both in the Platonic Ideas and in ideal numbers; the work is to a considerable degree a polemic against Pythagorean and Platonic conceptions. Mathematical objects, Aristotle holds, cannot exist as distinct substances either in or apart from sensible things; they can be separated only in thought. Number is consequently neither the efficient, material, formal, nor final cause of things. As becomes evident especially in the last section of the *Metaphysics,* this consideration destroys the harmony of the spheres.

A detailed refutation of the notion of the harmony of the spheres is found in *On the Heavens.*[7] Cosmic harmony is taken quite literally to be sounding music, and this interpretation itself—which is adopted without a word of justification—is characteristic of Aristotle. The disproof is then very simple, although it is faulty for all that; but to disprove the tones misses the point: the music can still be there, and indeed the concept in no way stands or falls with the existence of actual sonority.

Nor does a scientific attitude in itself contradict the idea, for it was scientific as well as poetical. The fundamental conceptions of Aristotle's metaphysics would have come to grips with cosmic harmony on its true merits, but *On the Heavens* has a simpler and more superficial argument, for it disposes merely with the secondary manifestation of sounding music. Such a disturbance would deafen us or at least cause great physical destruction; and Aristotle cites the analogous case of thunder; not knowing about the absence of air in space he obviously could not suspect his error. He goes on to take the absence of sound as evidence for his contention that the heavenly bodies are not detached objects but are imbedded in spheres, and here he does not realize that sound could result as well from the friction of a rotating sphere with the surrounding air as from the passage through air of a solid body. In the actual terms of Aristotle's argument, the absence of sound is taken as evidence that the motion of the stars is not self-caused, since it supposedly demonstrates that they are carried around by spheres; that their motion could have an external cause even if the stars were detached bodies his physics is unable to conceive, although inertia, to be sure, would not account for a motion assumed to be eternal.

Harmonic skepticism is again evident with respect to the soul, both in the treatise *On the Soul* and in the fragmentary dialogue *Eudemus*.[8] Aristotle is at one with Socrates in denying that the soul is a harmony of the body, a thesis advanced, as we have seen, by a pupil of Philolaus in the *Phaedo*. In addition, *On the Soul* firmly denies that the movements of the soul have anything to do with the heavenly bodies, and this would make it impossible to adduce a parallel with the cosmos in support of an intrinsic psychical harmony.

Yet strangely enough, harmonic conceptions play an exceedingly large part in Aristotle's philosophy. Confined to the physical or even the conceptual world, they have lost almost nothing of their scope. The important point is that they have no transcendental status, but are found in physics and mathematics and in the practical and productive sciences.

Aristotle does not believe in the Platonic harmony of the cosmos or the soul, nor does he believe that the presence of the same mathematical relationships in two phenomena has any real bearing on the interconnection or nature of these phenomena: it does not make them basically the same or even importantly similar. This follows from the fact that the two are not manifestations of a single independently existent idea or pattern, but are separate substances each with its own form, which is not that of any mathematical object. That the same mathematical order can be abstracted by thought from both is then simply due to some relatively extrinsic feature of their constitution; the agreement may be scientifically useful, but it is ontologically unimportant. By the same token, harmonic relationships are themselves not specifically musical; they are not of the nature of music, but are found in music as they may be found elsewhere. Thus harmonic order is not characteristic of the world, nor is it a metaphysically significant property of the phenomena from which it can be abstracted; the conjunction of these two circumstances completely divests music of its deeper importance and leaves it as a manifestation belonging no longer to metaphysics but to the sciences of physics and psychology, and with a peculiar but unexplained power to penetrate the soul, as Aristotle acknowledges in the *Politics.*

Harmony is officially deposed, but it is not completely evicted, and inconsistently, it still preserves traces of its Pythagorean significance. This can be seen in Aristotle's examination of sensation and its objects. One of the treatises that make up the *Parva Naturalia,* a group that follows after *On the Soul,* is called *On Sense and Sensible Objects,* and deals actually with the psychology of sensation in its relation to physics. A problem treated in detail is that of the mixture of sensations; another is that of their divisibility, or more specifically, of increments and fundamental sensations. Aristotle holds that since the objects of sensation are infinitely divisible, the sensations themselves must also be. Very small increments are not imperceptible but potentially perceptible, and are made actually so by aggregation, a conception that is applied elsewhere to the diesis. The range of sensations within a given sensory mode can be accounted for by the mixture of a few basic sensations, but still more fundamentally it is due to the combination of two extreme and contrary sensations—high and low, white and black, sweet and bitter—for the basic sensations themselves arise in this way. Blends or combinations of the contraries, such as high with low, result in a fixed number of intermediate species.

Here the theoretical justification is confused, but it is clear that harmonic theory and the analogy with music play an important role, and that Aristotle subscribes in considerable degree to correspondences between the senses. In general there are seven basic sensations within each mode; these are at any rate the chief blends and the ones that give pleasure. They correspond to the intervals of the musical scale and are similarly the result of definite, small-number ratios of combination. Other blends, not in simple and definite ratios, produce less pleasurable and less clear sensations; impure colors, for example, are the result of the complex or incommensurable relationships of their components, white and black.

On Sense and Sensible Objects obviously contains the kind of harmonic thought that is based on a belief in the metaphysical importance of harmony; this is evident not only in the explanation of the limited number of basic sensations, but also in the very conception of a duality underlying each sensory mode and giving rise by various harmonizations to the diverse phenomena of that sense. The same underlying mechanism explains why Aristotle regards the human voice as a harmony;[9] a single sensory object is itself a mean, a blend of basic contraries.

Hearing is also a harmony, or a ratio, according to the discussion in *On the Soul;*[10] excess in high or low pains or destroys the sense, while a mixed constitution provides a better and more pleasant harmony. In general, this particular aspect of harmony, the conjunction or fitting together of two opposites, is a persistent feature of Aristotle's thought and is the only aspect of the older metaphysical view that he retains, although he attempts at the same time to explain its generality on logical grounds. Also he denies to these contraries the status of absolutely first principles, for they must be predicated of something; this substratum is primary to them and has itself no contrary.

In the *Physics,*[11] contraries are translated into the sphere of language and generalized to cover the whole range of what is knowable and what is perceivable; they are held to be an inescapable feature of being, whether considered as static or changing, for anything has its contrary in that which is not itself. Harmony, for example, has a contrary in disharmony. But this is on a different plane from the notion of contraries as principles or elements; its importance lies not in showing Aristotle's belief in the significance of contraries, but only in reducing this significance to a matter of logical negation.

In his other treatises on physical science, however—in particular *On the Heavens, Meteorology,* and *On Generation and Corruption*—Aristotle relies heavily on the combination of contraries as a basic natural mechanism.[12] The four elements are the material causes acting in the sublunar region; each of them has its natural location, to which it tends to move in a straight line; and each of them is made up of a pair of contraries. Earth is constituted of dry and cold, water of moist and cold, air of moist and hot, and fire of dry and hot. More accurately, however, the contraries act in every case on some material substratum, so that each element has in reality three constituents.

It is interesting that the four causal factors that play the role of basic contraries in the production of the elements are themselves divided into two opposed types, namely active and passive, the active ones being hot and cold and the passive moist and dry. Furthermore, for any specific material entity, the underlying matter is made up ultimately of the two passive factors, while natural changes are caused by the intervention of the two active ones, which must also be in the proportion called for by any particular process of generation. Finally, this whole sublunar realm has its contrast in the celestial region, which is made up of the fifth element and characterized by the perfection of circular rather than straight-line motion. With more complex bodies, not only are the elements a material cause, but proportions of their combination enter as a formal cause, and as we have indicated, the proportions of the active properties become the formal basis of change.

The conception of harmony obviously plays an important part in the structure of the natural world. The four elements and the four properties are a Pythagorean heritage, the four causes may reflect the same tradition, and still other explanatory dualities are used, such as form and matter, and potentiality and actuality. The immense Pythagorean structure could not be razed in a day, but it is well on its way to becoming no more than a tool of scientific investigation, a particular relationship that is merely one among others, for the Aristotelian plan is drawn without any indications of metaphysical significance, and without suggesting that the structures and processes of the world are in any way those of music.

Harmony characterizes Aristotle's conception of man also; not only is it inherent in sense organs, as we have seen, so that they correspond in this respect to the nature of sensory objects, but it goes to make up bodily health and strength, which are characterized by harmonies of elements and their causal properties.[13] Even physical beauty is due to harmony, and bodily excellence of every type. Only the soul is excepted; it neither is nor contains harmony or number; *On the Soul* systematically opposes every notion of the *Timaeus*.

In respect of moral virtue itself, however, the *Nicomachean Ethics* assigns a vital role to proportion and harmony.[14] The good action is very much like a work of art; its materials are the emotions and tendencies aroused by a particular situation, and the man of practical wisdom will combine these in a proportioned manner to produce correct behavior. These ideal proportions become the standard for other people; the relative quantities of the constituents will differ for each person, but that blend which constitutes virtue will be a reasoned one determined with reference to the ideal case. If a man has an unusually impulsive tendency to react with violence, for example, or is especially quick to be moved to anger, the proportions of this tendency or of this feeling that must be allowed to enter a particular decision and action, although they are determined partly by reference to the proportions in the actions of an ideal agent, will be lower down along the range of reaction and feeling than they are in the model instance by an amount that depends on the relation between the given agent and the ideal one with respect to the attributes in question. The action is thus determined by a mean of relative nature which involves the notions of proportion and of a balanced mixture of constituents.

With the reservation that Aristotle's conception is not so peculiarly dominated by the notion of an ideal harmony, it is otherwise quite like an elaboration of the description of the good in Plato's *Philebus*. The moral action, then, is a composite of material and form; the material, consisting of feelings and impulses, is in itself indefinite and neither good nor bad; it is in the form, the determinate proportions in which the constituents are combined, that the value of the act resides. Each of these constituents must participate in a mean degree which is relative for a given agent in a given set of circumstances. The time of the event, the people involved, the particular intention of the act, the manner in which it is consummated, the nature of the provocation: all are relevant to the determination. And the appropriateness must also be measured by the responses of the ideal agent. On this basis the total pattern manifested in the act can be constructed. For any constituent the mean is relative but at the same time absolute, because given the particular context, the form is determined by rule and proportion and is consequently unique. There is only one correct solution, one good action, for each moral situation.

Also conforming to harmonic notions is Aristotle's typical conception of the constituents of conduct, for each of these has a range between two contraries, such as those of pleasure and pain or of confidence and fear; at any rate, this is the nature of those passions and actions that admit of a mean, and these are the ones that come into question in applying rational principles to the form of moral behavior. Both the good action and the purposive state of character that is productive of this action may be described in identical fashion; that is to say, moral virtue also involves limitation by a rational principle or a right proportion, and it also has the nature of a mean that is relative to the agent. The man of practical wisdom is able to choose the proportion that correctly limits or determines the mean for any individual action because he knows the nature of the ultimate good in life, and this highest value is the standard for all the others; the right proportion for action in each case is one of the elements that goes to construct the best life, and knowledge of the whole pattern, of the master formula, implies the ability to determine its details. Furthermore, the form of the best life, or the pattern of any particular species of good conduct, is in itself the theory of behavior, or practical wisdom; the proportion that makes an action good by determining the proper amount of emotion is also a principle of practical knowledge.

Aristotle's conception of justice, like that of any particular virtue, is also based on the notion of mean value. It is especially clear in this case, however, that mathematical proportion is a scientific tool rather than an inherent or harmonic characteristic of justice. Other virtues are means between two opposed vices that represent the extremes of excess and defect; but justice is a mean in a different sense, for a deviation from it in either direction involves both excess and defect simultaneously. In its general sense, justice encompasses and includes every virtue; it is coincident with the whole of civic virtue. But justice has a special sense in which it designates a particular virtue of fairness, and in this sense it involves either equitable shares, or where wrong has been done, equitable redress. Here Aristotle rejects reciprocation as defining the nature of justice, and has recourse instead to concepts of proportion. Equitable shares are governed by a geometrical proportion, which assigns to two individuals amounts in the same ratio as that of their legal statuses. Redress, on the other hand, is determined by an arithmetical proportion, and consists in restoring to the injured party an amount given by the arithmetic mean between the gain and loss due to the initial inequity.

In Aristotle's ethical philosophy of music, imitation remains a

central determinant, although it has lost a certain amount of its commanding influence. Unfortunately the second part of the *Poetics,*
which undoubtedly dealt with melic poetry, has not come down to
us, but the initial discussion makes it clear that imitation was a
general feature of art.[15] Unlike Plato, however, Aristotle does not
have a low regard for imitation; he is not concerned with its removal from reality, but finds instead that it is natural to man, that it
teaches him, and that it gives him delight. Thus art is given a basis
in human nature and is regarded as inherently ethical and pleasurable; our delight in it, however, is not due to its sensuous properties
but to a delight in learning. Aristotle discusses imitation in detail,
taking up in turn its media, its model (men in action), and its
manner (a concept that can be illustrated by narration and acting,
for example). In the *Republic,* Plato finds the distinction between
narration and acting to be important in determining the ethical
value of art, but apart from the educational value of imitation, the
concept is free from moral issues in Aristotle's treatment; he characteristically confines himself to the phenomenon itself, excluding
from his science even the problem of its ontological status.

The ethical scheme of Aristotle conceives the best life as the life of
virtuous actions; in this the nature of man as a compound of body
and soul is most fully expressed. Less valuable are play, amusement,
and the enjoyment of art, for these are not purposeless, but serve the
end of renewed ability to work. Still higher in value than virtuous
action, on the other hand, is theoretical contemplation; this is an
activity of the divine element in man, and it brings perfect felicity.
The function of the state is to make the best life possible, so that
the *Politics* supplements and implements the *Ethics;* more particularly, every citizen should be molded to suit the form of government
under which he lives: in its educational function, the state must give
rise to a congruent way of life. Even in Plato there is more than one
program of studies and more than one concept of musical value; but
for Aristotle the horizon is noticeably widened to go beyond educa-

tion in the strict sense of the word and encompass functions of music that no longer have their explanation in imitation.[16] The larger scope appears at once in the aporia that opens the musical discussion of the *Politics:* what is the aim of education? is it utility, virtue, or higher knowledge? Aristotle's conception of music encompasses all three of these goals and finds room for still other musical tasks that exceed the province of ethics altogether.

In the training of young children, knowledge that vulgarizes is to be excluded. Only the liberal arts are to be imparted; but these, too, can have illiberal effects if they are learned either with a view to perfection or for the sake of other people. Among the customary branches of lower education, reading, writing, and drawing are primarily useful, although reading and drawing have other benefits as well. Gymnastics, on the other hand, serve the end of virtue, for they inculcate courage; at the same time they provide an excellent example of how an art becomes illiberal when it is studied to excess, for under such conditions they will not produce courage at all, but instead injure the body and exhaust the constitution.

On the general principle that practice should precede theory, Aristotle holds that the body should be trained before the mind. He also believes that mental and physical pursuits interfere with one another and should not be undertaken simultaneously. These notions contrast sharply with those of Plato, who operates with the broader concept of training the soul (a process he would commence even in the prenatal stage) and who seeks the complementary effect of music and gymnastics and their continual harmonization.

As far as music is concerned, Aristotle is quite aware of its position as the prototype of liberal education. The original and chief reason it became a branch of lower education was to achieve the ultimate objective of higher knowledge, which is broadly construed as encompassing both intellectual activity and intellectual enjoyment. The goal is to use leisure well, the pursuit is disinterested, and the pleasurable aspect is designated as an end and not a means. But

music has a more humble role as well, since it is cultivated for amusement, a lower kind of pleasure which we must regard as a medicine
to be introduced only at suitable times. Here it provides a needed
respite from undertakings of more concrete value, permitting us to
return to these refreshed and thus more efficient. Finally music serves
the end of virtue, since it forms our minds and habituates us to true
pleasures; it acts, in other words, to make virtue pleasurable.

But is it necessary for us to learn music ourselves in order to
secure its values? Perhaps we can be listeners only, and leave performance to professionals. Zeus does not sing or play, and no freeman would do so unless he were jesting or drunk; indeed professional performers are vulgar. Is it possible, in spite of this, that performance has a place in education? Amusement and relaxation are
certainly not attached to the process of learning, which is actually a
matter of difficulty and effort, and in later life, at any rate, they are
easily secured by listening to others. It would make as much sense to
learn cookery. Virtue, too, seems to be as well obtained by listening
as by performance. And similarly intellectual enjoyment, along with
correct judgment, can doubtless be secured simply by listening. Furthermore children are still imperfect, and intellectual enjoyment,
which is an end in itself, is not really appropriate to them.

Yet Aristotle decides the question in favor of performance, contradicting the arguments he has just advanced and urging that
children be taught to sing and play: the actual practice of the art
substantially increases its influence on the character; those who do
not perform cannot be good judges of the performance of others
(which really means also that they cannot derive the highest intellectual enjoyment from music); and finally children should have
something to do, for a young thing cannot be quiet, and education can
be compared to the toys of still younger children.

Thus in early education, performance appears to further all the
ends of music; it serves virtue, intellectual enjoyment, and play,
functions designated as *paideia, diagoge,* and *paidia.* Although no

case is made explicitly for its value as amusement, we can see nothing else in its advantage in satisfying the natural impulse to activity, for this is certainly amusement and relaxation during the time of education. An equally strong argument could be presented for the value of performance as play in later life, but this would be embarrassing to Aristotle's general position. In addition, performance would doubtless be serviceable to catharsis, a musical function taken up subsequently. Sufficient reason is adduced in any event for the introduction of performance into education.

Perhaps the greatest strength of Aristotle's philosophy of music resides in the detailed working out of the principles of its use; there is a broad consideration of the variety of factors that influence the problem and a wise freedom from dogmatism. What seems wrong from one point of view, Aristotle shows, can be valuable from another; moreover he is always conscious of the need for moderation, as though musical study contained a particularly great danger of vulgarization.

The questions he examines are essentially those of appropriateness: to what extent should freemen study music? and what melodies and rhythms and instruments should they be permitted to use? Practice in performance should begin at an early age so that students learn to appreciate what is good and to delight in it; the aim determines the correct extent of the study: it must continue until a merely sensuous delight in music gives way to an informed and specific pleasure in noble melodies and rhythms, but must then come to a halt before aspiring to virtuosity.

Professional performance means vulgarization, for a reason Aristotle has already discussed: the professional practices for the sake of others, not for his own improvement; he is vulgarized because his purpose is bad. The vulgarity of the audience calls forth music that is vulgar and thus vulgarizes the performer also. The study of music should not interfere with the serious concerns of later life; it should not make the body unfit for gymnastics or for later studies. These would again spell vulgarization; they are avoided by assigning musical education to early years and by avoiding excess.

In general, music will become illiberal either if it is practiced for the sake of others or if it interferes with other liberal pursuits. Aristotle's view of the permissible use of instruments follows from the same considerations: those requiring great skill or designed solely to give pleasure to the hearer are to be excluded. The aulos is objectionable for both these reasons, and also because it is exciting and thus does not express moral character. But the indictment of the instrument continues: it distorts the face, it prevents the use of the voice, and it contributes nothing to the mind. Thus after inventing it Athena cast it away. It is typical of Aristotle, however, that he is still able to find a proper use for the aulos; although excluded from education, it is suitable for the cathartic relief of passion, a function that preserves the medical application of music to purge the soul.

In his discussion of permissible modes, Aristotle leaves the question of performance behind; his remarks presumably apply to listening also. The educational aim now clearly gives way to a wider purpose, and the philosopher declares that music should be studied not for the sake of one but of many benefits: for moral cultivation, purgation, intellectual virtue, and recreation and relaxation—*paideia, katharsis, diagoge,* and *paidia* and *anapausis.* Also each age of life and each class of society has its own needs. The result is that no mode can be absolutely excluded; the problem is simply to apply them all correctly.

The breadth of the conception is comparable to that of Plato's *Laws;* the severity of the *Republic* is due to the fact that it follows a narrower purpose. The variety of the objectives considered by Aristotle provides occasions of use for modes and melodies that are ethical, active, and passionate or inspiring; even modes that are perverted and melodies that are highly strung and unnaturally colored are suitable for the recreation of the vulgar crowd, while the relaxed modes are appropriate for old men. Any mode that possesses order and ethos and is suited to young children is also of value for the aged. The distinctions in modal use actually vary with the purpose or function of the music, with the age of the people in question, with the musical activity (whether performing or listening), and with personality and social-intellectual status.

Of the three purposes of education—utility, moral cultivation, and intellectual virtue (or higher knowledge)—music clearly serves the latter two: *paideia* and *diagoge*. In furthering pleasure, however, it also serves the end of utility, for pleasure is not always purposeless: if *paidia* is play, recreation, or amusement pure and simple, *anapausis* is relaxation, or amusement for the sake of renewed efficiency in work. *Diagoge* is to be distinguished from both of these; both contain pleasure, which has unfortunately in itself been made the end of music; but *diagoge* is a higher kind of pleasure, and it also contains an ethical component.[17] Lower forms of pleasure are quite liable to be mistaken for ultimate goods, since these also, as existing for their own sake, must have a certain pleasure attached to them.

To the three announced functions of music, a fourth is subsequently added—that of *katharsis*—but his interest in preserving a triple division leads Aristotle to group *diagoge* together with *paidia-anapausis*, just as it is grouped with them in the less valuable life of pleasure discussed in the *Nicomachean Ethics*. Thus *paideia, paidia-anapausis, diagoge* becomes *paideia, paidia-anapausis-diagoge, katharsis*. To this latter division there corresponds roughly the triple division of melodies or modes: ethical, practical, passionate. But even if we consider amusement solely as recuperation for renewed action, the practical melodies—or those of action—would not seem specifically appropriate to such a function. This division of modes, however, also corresponds with the classification in the *Poetics* of the objects of imitation: *ethos, praxis, pathos*.

Melodies, or modes, are alternatively divided into moderate, enthusiastic, sad, and relaxed, and these types correspond somewhat more closely to the functions of music. The moderate or temperate

(Dorian) serves the function of moral cultivation, which applies to youth and involves performance; the other functions, which apply to adults and involve listening, are served by the enthusiastic type (Phrygian), for *katharsis,* and by the sad and relaxed types, along with those that are perverted and highly strung, for *paidia, anapausis,* and *diagoge,* although here it becomes difficult to justify the correspondence in detail. Listening, which presumably would realize all the functions of music except possibly that of *paideia,* will employ not only the modes of action and of passion, but also those of relaxed character (for the old and the very young) and of unnatural character (for the vulgar). Thus in a general way, the melodic types further the various musical functions, manifesting the flexibility of ethical standards in their correspondence with age and social status.

In addition Aristotle does not present us with a closed system: modes are to be included that are approved by philosophers with a musical education. The outlined program in the *Politics* is not completed by a discussion of the use of rhythms, but Aristotle's treatment of modes makes his outlook clear and permits us to guess what his rhythmical theories would be like. The promise to investigate the relative importance of melody and rhythm in music is also not fulfilled. But the text that has come down to us is not complete, and curiously, just as in the *Poetics,* the part that has been lost concerned music. In any event, Aristotle's discussion is intended to be a general one; he leans on the fact that the subject has been very well treated by others. It is obvious, nevertheless, that although Aristotle has an elevated view of music, he is equally aware of its humbler values and its diversity of use. Thus his examination of music deals as much with its general aesthetic properties as with its ethical ones.

In its universality of function, music appears to make a contribution to each of the three activities that Aristotle considers at the conclusion of the *Ethics* as possible components of the best life. Virtuous activity is furthered by musical *paideia,* amusement by *paidia, anapausis,* and *diagoge,* and contemplation by *diagoge* also. Only *katharsis* is left without application, although it has some connection both with ascetic virtue and with enjoyment. The highest happiness of contemplation corresponds to Plato's dialectic; is it also in some sense a hymn?

There can be no doubt that just as the artistic form of the dialogue was discarded by Aristotle, so philosophy has completely lost its musical nature; but in *diagoge,* on the other hand, music has taken on a philosophic character, and to classify it among the amusements of the *Ethics* is probably to do it an injustice. *Diagoge* is really *eleutherios diagoge,* a way of life fit for a freeman; it represents an ideal of culture and scientific leisure as opposed to pure play, which Aristotle consistently associated with *anapausis,* relaxation that was not disinterested but served the higher purpose of abetting virtuous activity. Thus *diagoge* has something of the purposeless quality of the highest life of theoretical contemplation; if it is Aristotle's distinctive contribution to musical ethics and aesthetics, it is also a secularization of the religious ideal of Plato's *Laws*—the life of peace, which as we have seen is a transfiguration of play. The ceremonial motif of the choral dance has given way to the enjoyment of the cultivated listener, to a kind of theoretical contemplation of music.

In the *Laws* and the *Republic* the goal of *paideia* is the love and enjoyment of beauty, not just of ideal but of sensuous beauty as well; but the aesthetics is basically ethical in that pleasure is taken only in the music of virtue and culture. In dispensing with this explicit religious and ethical basis and substituting a more purely philosophic ideal and a purposelessness in principle, Aristotle shifts the balance in favor of aesthetics, especially as he also discards Plato's antisensuous tendency. By contrast, the *Republic* is antisensuous, the *Laws* cultivates a religious setting and seeks to create pleasure in hymns, in the music of virtue, even for adults to whom the paideutic function is no longer relevant, the *Timaeus* finds pleasure in a pure music, but one that still owes its beauty to an ethical-intellectual character; and in all three dialogues, harmonics is superior to music in providing a higher pleasure divorced from sense.

Only in the ritual hymns of the leisured life of peace in the *Laws* do we approach Aristotle's conception, for music here partakes as much of disinterested sensuous enjoyment as Plato's fundamental ethical outlook could countenance. Music may mold the child's play and man be a plaything of the gods, but the child's play is converted to ethical ends and a sad necessity compels man to regard his life seriously—that is, in a moral light.

Within the field of rhetoric, which was less intimately allied to morality than politics, a more purely aesthetic theory of music expressed itself; it was directed, however, not to contemplation but to the emotional impact of music. Here the expansive tendencies of Aristotle's ethical conceptions of music, their freedom from a metaphysical basis in harmony, and the variety of musical influences they encompassed all found a natural fulfillment. The parallel between music and oratory is a natural one, but in classical antiquity it was very nearly an equivalence rather than an analogy, for the musical character of formal speech was literal. Socrates summons up the notion of inspiration and invokes the Muses in the creation of his first oration in the *Phaedrus*.[18] By way of a more formal correspondence between the two arts, the preamble to the written laws of the state in Plato's *Laws* is compared to the prelude of the musical *nomos:* [19] it has the same function of setting the character and spirit of what follows.

The fundamental relationship between oratory and music is found in the swaying of the feelings; this presupposes an analysis of the nature and variety of feelings, just as the less transient effects on character in musical ethics are based on an analysis of the soul. But there are formal analogies between the two fields also, which can be instructive to both musical and rhetorical theory. Finally, music is a servant of oratory not only in reinforcing its emotional effects but in the training of the orator as well, where its effects are both mechanical, in the control and power of the voice, and more fundamental, in molding the character of the speaker so that he represents rhetoric in its nobler aspect rather than as a field of false persuasion. Music can even supply the orator with subject matter, both for individual figures and for whole speeches, whether of praise or of legal argument. In the laudatory address, rhetoric takes over the chief traditional topic of music, and in the oration in praise of music, the dual role of music may be responsible for the popularity and persistence of the genre. The function of music in the education of the speaker involves a complete reorientation of educational ideals which was consummated only in late antiquity; oratory took its place in the series of goals for which music had been found valuable: military prowess and valor, aristocratic leisure, the ritual basis of social coherence, philosophy, and disinterested intellectual pleasure.

Of the two schools of rhetoric which developed in the fifth century B.C., the eastern or Ionian one concentrated on precision of style and was therefore less inclined to incorporate musical factors. The Sicilian school, however, emphasized stylistic beauty. The Sophist and rhetorician Thrasymachus of Chalcedon, who represented this school in the second half of the century, is reputedly the first to have directed attention to the importance of oral delivery. His sentences were rounded off in periods marked by a paeonic rhythm at the beginning and end. The use of paeonic rhythm was supported not only by Aristotle but also by the Sophist Theodectes of Phaselis in Pamphylia, a tragic poet and rhetorician active in the middle of the fourth century who believed that prose should in general be rhythmical although not metrical.

It is only with Aristotle, however, that there is preserved a detailed statement of the musical features of rhetoric, which is found in Book III of his *Rhetoric*. In Book II, Aristotle takes up the importance of a knowledge of the emotions, in a discussion which must be regarded as basic to the affective aesthetics of music even though it is directed solely to the rhetorician. The psychological description of the emotions is accompanied by a discussion of the variety of human character and personality in its dependence upon feeling, period of life, wealth and station, and habits, virtues, and vices. Each emotion is analyzed with respect to its causes, the other people it implicates, and the general frame of mind it represents. Aristotle discusses in turn anger and mildness, love and hatred, fear, shame and shamelessness, benevolence, pity, indignation, envy, emulation, and contempt.

More specifically musical are the discussions of delivery, style, and form in Book III. Delivery is especially illustrative of the close relationship of music and oratory as revealed in the development of the two arts. Aristotle points out the musical parallel himself: the performer, whether actor or rhapsodist, was also the composer, and there was thus no need for a theoretical examination of performance. The situation had changed only recently—a manifestation of increasing specialization—and the change was presumably a forecast of the same development in oratory, although Aristotle does not discuss the separation of writer and speaker in this field. He disapproves of the recent stress on oratorical delivery, however, and indeed on style itself; these are vulgar, and are important only because of the corruption of the listeners. Facts alone should suffice; but style is unfortunately necessary in order for us to achieve the aim of rhetoric, which is to influence opinion. There is a higher standard, however; what is necessary is not the same as what is right. Although the parallel remains implicit, the emphasis on delivery and effect that concerns Aristotle so deeply cannot fail to remind us of the stress in music and poetry on virtuosity, on impressing the audience in a bid for applause instead of concentrating on truth and virtue.

Delivery is largely musical; it concerns the voice and the manner of employing it, the utilization of pitch and rhythm in accordance with the content of the speech. "For there are three qualities that are considered—volume, harmony, rhythm. Those who use these properly nearly always carry off the prizes in dramatic contests, and as at the present day actors have greater influence on the stage than the poets, it is the same in political contests, owing to the corruptness of our forms of governments." [20]

The connection with music is quite explicit, and it is reinforced by the theory of the ethical and political influence of music; the two fields become related expressions of the same cultural decline. At best, style does serve the purpose of clarity; but distinctions of style are really not of importance, for they concern display and are directed simply to the pleasure of the listener. No regard is paid to them, Aristotle cleverly points out, in the teaching of geometry. It is unfortunate, he finds, that the effect of a speech depends more on style than on sense. In attending to style and delivery poetry may have led the way, but that does not imply that oratory must follow poetic style in detail; as a matter of fact, in tragedy we have an instance in which poetry has followed speech, turning to iambic meter because this is the species closest to prose. Oratory, of course, should have a distinctive style, yet it should make use largely of the words and metaphors of ordinary speech. On the other hand, the metaphors are to be evaluated in terms of the musical standard of euphony; this criterion curiously applies not only to the words of the metaphor themselves but also to any metaphorical physical events that are sonorous: a comparison is spoiled if it refers to harsh sounds.

Rhetoric is also close to music in matters of stylistic propriety; this is true even in the requirement that style must be proportionate to subject, but it is more noticeably the case in the demand that it be both emotional, so as to create the feeling of sympathy, and ethical, so as to express character. The fundamental tenet behind the ethical requirement—that every moral nature has an appropriate linguistic expression—also has a direct parallel in music.

Although meter will prevent the orator from being persuasive and will distract the attention of the listener, oratorical prose should certainly have rhythm; indeed the absence of rhythm creates obscurity and unpleasantness. Heroic rhythm is too dignified, iambic too ordinary, and trochaic too like a comic dance; but the paeonic is suitable both to the beginning of sentences, where the type in which the long syllable precedes the three short ones is appropriate, and to the end, which calls for the other type in which the long syllable comes last.

Another rhythmical feature is the use of a periodic rather than a continuous style, the periods consisting of either one or several members. And a specifically sonorous device is that of *paramoiosis:* similarity of sound either at the beginning or at the end of a sentence. As opposed to the written, deliberative, forensic, and epideictic styles, the one best suited to declamation is the agonistic; appropriately, it is this style that will be either ethical or pathetic.

Finally musical factors enter into the arrangement of a speech and the functions of its various parts. The arrangement is basically that of statement and proof, although these may be preceded by an exordium and followed by an epilogue. The exordium is like the prelude in aulos playing and the prologue in poetry. In an epideictic speech in particular (although this is the style best adapted to writing) it resembles the musical prelude and is connected with the body of the speech by the keynote, which is derived from the topics of praise or blame. The narrative should be ethical and should show the moral purpose and the various moral traits that accompany each particular character; also the speaker should react to the emotional features. Since maxims are ethical, they are permissible in both the narrative and the proof. In deliberative oratory, which because it deals with an unknown future is more difficult than forensic, the speech should be both demonstrative and ethical if the speaker has enthymemes available; if not he should speak only ethically. The epilogue or peroration includes the function of making the listener favorable to the speaker and unfavorable to the opponent; it also has the more or less musical task of putting the listener into an emotional frame of mind.

But rhetoric reveals only an extreme of the change that Aristotle effected generally in musical ethics; the highly theoretical conception of Plato was renounced in favor of a closer approach to the realities of practice, a parallel of the fact that the powerful motivation provided by social thought directed to an ideal polis was no longer possible. At the same time, the fractionation of music permitted informed listening to take the place of musical participation, with a resultant relaxation and broadening of the ethical demands made upon music. The new freedom of art from moral and political considerations was mirrored in philosophy, where Aristotle's *Poetics* subjected artistic problems and properties to an independent examination. Full recognition could be given to every aspect of music, a possibility facilitated by the advantages of a scientific attitude over a social one in respect of impartiality. Music in the service of *paideia,* with its appropriate modes and rhythms, was after all only one kind of music among many. The highest values now were to be found in leisure, for in thought and the activities approximating it the potentiality of man achieved fulfillment.

Yet much remained unchanged in Aristotle's philosophy; the ethical foundation was expanded but not outgrown; it still supported the main weight of the structure. The greatest loss of stability it suffered was due to the lack of a harmonic underpinning. "There seems to be in us a sort of affinity to musical modes and rhythms, which makes some philosophers say that the soul is a tuning, others, that it possesses tuning." [21] But this is as far as Aristotle will go. The fragment found in the Pseudo-Plutarch *On Music,*[22] which speaks of the divine nature of harmony, forms a curious exception to his attitude. But harmonic skepticism may have helped to produce the breadth of his ethical conceptions. Even *katharsis* has a place among the effects of music instead of standing apart from the rest as it does in Plato; although it may be a necessary preliminary to the harmonious applications of music, it certainly does not itself act by means of harmony or order; since it brings pleasure, however, Aristotle does not discard it. Indeed a positive attitude toward pleasure is largely responsible for the variety of musical influences he will accept; music is not just good or bad: its diversity at times approaches ethical indifference, and a range of specifically musical values.

Imitation is also both retained and altered. Its model remains human action and character, including now even what is ugly; but instead of turning to individual things it seeks out their ideal and general nature, a process quite different, however, from the revelation of an eternal reality behind them. Also instrumental music is no longer objectionably vague; achieving philosophical recognition, it becomes in Aristotle's view peculiarly capable of imitating character as well as of forming it. Most important of all is the connection of imitation with knowledge; it is because we learn from art that we take pleasure in it; our whole reaction is made dependent upon the object imitated: "the habit of feeling pleasure or pain at mere representations is not far removed from the same feeling about realities." [23]

Now if this continues the subordination of aesthetics to epistemology and perpetuates the fateful neglect of specifically aesthetic values, we cannot fail to recognize the radical difference between the view of Aristotle and that of Plato, for the knowledge provided by art is no longer regarded as spurious or even inferior but has become a source of educational value. Plato's sad realization of the mediate character of knowledge is fully accepted and confirmed; art is not a valueless copy of reality, but as an affair of imitation, serves actually to illuminate an inescapable feature of human thought. Peculiarly aesthetic properties may still be neglected, but in connecting art with the most godlike of human activities, Aristotle joined Plato in ensuring its future philosophical importance.

The Peripatetic philosophy of music was determined not only by

Aristotle's ethical and aesthetic theories but also by his conception of harmony. If number was only an abstraction from objects made by thought and not an independent existent, harmonic form had still less autonomy, for harmonics was a discipline dependent upon arithmetic, and, as we have seen, it dealt with properties that could not even be fully abstracted from physical objects. Acoustic structure was investigated not in its acoustic nature, of course, but only to the extent that it could be represented mathematically; yet the science gives a true picture of the Aristotelian conception of music as an indissoluble compound of material and form. In sense as well as thought it is form that is abstracted, and again there can be no separation, for the actuality of sound is audibility. Just as the concept is the simultaneous realization of the human mind and the rational nature of the world, so the potentialities of sense organ and sound source have a single actuality in harmonic form that is heard. Thus in its own way, Peripatetic musical philosophy is compounded of the meeting of aesthetic and harmonic concepts, but music is an essential substance, a fusion, and not an appearance that participates in ontologic form.

In respect of the source of music, Aristotle accepts and expands Plato's conception that it arises from innate human capacity. Harmony and rhythm are instinctively imposed on the spontaneous production of sound and motion that man manifests in common with animals. But in Aristotle's view imitation is also inherent in human nature; both in its aesthetic properties and its relation to the world music is a natural expression of man. This is a logical counterpart, if it is not the actual basis, of its influence, for we respond to musical imitations very much as we respond to nonimitative situations; there is also no artificiality involved in the effect of music. Our souls undergo a change, so that the end of music is the same as its source. Aristotle is quite definite in his descriptions of the essential reality of music; melody, rhythm, and dance are in themselves natural imitations of character, emotion, and action, and our experience in listening to music reveals that "they hardly fall short of the actual affections." [24]

Given this secure basis in experience, which complements its monistic metaphysical constitution, music succeeds to importance for the sake of its own properties rather than its wider connections. The specialized and scientific interest of Aristotelian musical thought follows as a matter of course; every physical and qualitative attribute of sound is significant, and the details of musical acoustics, physiology, psychology, and theory are carefully examined.

A concern with the qualitative and biological rather than the mathematical aspects of tone is also an understandable idiosyncrasy of Peripatetic scientific tracts. The comprehensive treatment of sensation in Aristotle's *On the Soul* includes analyses of the physics of sound and of the physiology of the ear and the voice; its main interest is in the nature of hearing. Voice and ear correspond; like the lyre, they are both ratios or harmonies, an adjustment or balance of contraries, and the single tone that actualizes the potentialities of both is thus also a concord. Harmony is the presence of a mean, and excess of high or low will destroy hearing.

It is typical that pitch is treated in congruence with the qualities of the other senses and not as a measurable or mathematical attribute. Acute and grave are metaphors transferred from touch, Aristotle tells us. "There seems to be a sort of parallelism between what is acute or grave to hearing and what is sharp or blunt to touch; what is sharp as it were stabs, while what is blunt pushes, the one producing its effect in a short, the other in a long time, so that the one is quick, the other slow." [25] The difference in the qualities is due to speed of motion in both senses, but it is not subjected to quantitative description; indeed Greek music reserves the quantitative concepts high and low for the more obviously physical relationships of the strings of the lyre, and it is with these that the precise measurements of the musical system are concerned.

The Peripatetic outlook, however, is psychological, and does not take account of physical magnitude; ultimately this is due to the fact that music is a specific and concrete phenomenon; harmony is not a cosmic manifestation, and tone as an expression of the external world is of less interest than the voice as an expression of the human soul.

If this distinction is pursued, it will suggest that the Pythagorean and Platonic conception applied a physical outlook to the soul, treating it quantitatively in terms of number and figure, while the Aristotelian conception applied a biological outlook to the physical world, neglecting mathematics even where it was most obviously useful. Thus natural sounds also have a qualitative interest, actualizing the potentialities of sound that exist in porosity or hardness, in the nature of the material, rather than in length.

These characteristics of *On the Soul* are further exemplified in the *Generation of Animals,* which discusses the nature of the voice and of sound.[26] Vocal quality is subjected to close observation and to physiological and physical explanation; even pitch takes its place among the qualitative attributes. Thus voices are described as low and high, big and small, smooth and rough, flexible and inflexible. Pitch depends upon the relationship of quantity between the agent and what is moved, but this basis is not treated mathematically or measured in any way, and the discussion deals exclusively with pitch as a reflection of age, species of animal, sex, health or sickness, castration, and even climate of habitat, for hot breath is supposedly responsible for low tones both in voices and in musical instruments.

Since man alone uses the voice as the material for rational speech, he possesses the vocal faculty in an exceptional degree; for this reason the pitch difference due to sex is most noticeable in the human voice. "Further, a deep voice seems to be the mark of a nobler nature, and in melodies, too, that which is deep-pitched is better than the high-pitched, since deepness is a form of superiority, and it is in superiority that betterness resides. In fact, however, deep and high pitch of the voice is a different matter from largeness and smallness of the voice." [27] The greater perfection of low tones is thus not a matter of size, but is clearly associated with the higher actuality of the adult as compared to the child. The qualitative aspects of tone—sharp and heavy, clear and obscure—are also discussed in the *Topics*,[28] in conjunction with the qualities found in other sensory modes.

In the tracts of the Peripatetic school following Aristotle—*On Things Heard, On Tones, Physiognomics,* and *Physical Problems*—this scientific interest in sound and hearing and the voice is continued. The early Peripatetic work *On Things Heard,* for example, discusses the production of sound, and is completely qualitative rather than mathematical in its descriptions. The qualities of sound are accounted for in terms of the constitution and motion of the physical sources; strong empirical interest and descriptive skill are quite apparent, and they result in observations that cast light on a peculiar qualitative phase of the history of science.

One of the advances of the Peripatetics was a more accurate appreciation of the nature of acoustic vibration and its effect on the surrounding air. Pitch had been connected with speed by both Archytas and Plato, but speed of propagation—which was conceived as a translatory motion of air—was not separated from rapidity of vibration or of the successive impulses at the ear. But with the important Academic and Peripatetic philosopher Heraclides Ponticus, the vibratory nature of sound was more clearly grasped, and the Pythagorean theory of music was provided with a new basis for the identification of number with pitch and for the explanation of the fusion of consonant tones.

Number no longer had to be connected with length (often in flagrant disagreement with empirical observations of wind instruments or vessels), nor did it have to appeal, in even greater contradiction with experience and measurement, to a basis in tension or the velocity of sound, but could claim instead a precise identification with the tonal impulses imparted through the air by a vibrating source, even if these were too rapid to be counted. This growing awareness of the physical nature of tone is found in *On Things Heard,* in the *Physical Problems,* and in the Pythagorean tract by Euclid, the *Section of the Canon.*

The scope of the *Physical Problems* makes it by far the most impressive work in the group of post-Aristotelian treatises bearing on music. Questions that are put more than once, sometimes with slight differences, indicate that we are dealing with what was probably a standard collection designed for Lyceum studies. Book XI undertakes to account for the varied qualitative differences of the human voice both acoustically and physiologically. Again lower tones are regarded as superior to higher ones; like men as compared to boys, they are more perfect and represent a more advanced degree of entelechy. Book XIX, the subject of which is given as "harmony," is much wider in range and of considerably greater philosophic value.

In addition to an understanding of the impulsive theory of tone and its connection with consonant fusion, the questions show a great deal of interest in the octave. "Why is the octave consonance the most beautiful? Why is the octave a pleasanter sound than the unison?" The octave is recognized as the interval uniquely suitable for polyphonic singing, and its lower tone is held to be the more important of the two.

But musical practice enters not only in connection with the octave, for the tract is concerned throughout with the aesthetic properties of music, and it seeks scientific explanations for psychological phenomena and the particularities of musical experience. "Why does everyone enjoy rhythm and melody and in general all consonance? Why do those who are sad and those who are enjoying themselves both make use of the aulos? Why do we listen with greater pleasure to music we know than to music we do not know? Why does irregularity in a song produce a tragic effect?"

Significantly, the ethical sphere is more poorly represented. "Why is neither the hypodorian nor hypophrygian mode used by the chorus in tragedy? Why is hearing the only perception which affects the moral character? Why are the *nomoi* which men sing so called?"

These questions have more of a historical cast; superseded by newer interests and made obsolete by a changed world, ethical concerns are retained only by the force of tradition. What the *Problems* clearly document is an astonishing growth in aesthetic awareness; beauty, pleasure, and feeling have become the center of interest.

Both of Aristotle's outstanding pupils, Aristoxenus and Theophrastus, were particularly interested in music. Aristoxenus is undoubtedly one of the greatest musical authorities of antiquity, combining a detailed technical knowledge of music with broader philosophic considerations. Study with Aristotle superimposed on earlier Pythagorean training produced highly distinctive musical views which were built on a theoretical base strong enough to ensure their persistence for centuries. Aristoxenus' consciousness of his originality is obtrusive, but it is undoubtedly justified; the various musical disciplines certainly existed before his time, but the new spirit in which he established them is of such importance that he is actually entitled to be regarded as their founder. At the same time, although he carries Aristotelian principles to their logical conclusion, he also goes beyond his master to create a fully aesthetic philosophy of music. Very little remains of his vast output; we have only an incomplete *Harmonics* and fragments of a *Rhythmics,* but much can be surmised from his huge influence as well as actually pieced together from the writings of Athenaeus, Pseudo-Plutarch, Cleonides, Aristides Quintilianus, and Bellermann's Anonymi. That he was still of interest in the late Middle Ages is indicated by Bryennius' formulation of his ideas in the fourteenth century.

The *Harmonics* we now possess actually comprises writings belonging to two types of treatise, *Principles* and *Elements,* the *Prin-*

ciples representing an Aristotelian approach to the science, and the *Elements*—a series of theorems with proofs—the Pythagorean or Euclidean aspect. Although harmonics is only one of the musical sciences, Aristoxenus regards it as the principal one; he takes pains to dissipate any illusions the prospective student might entertain about its nature, however; it will neither make him a musician nor improve his character.

In the course of his characteristically Aristotelian altercation with previous exponents of the discipline, it becomes clear that the theoretical likelihood of different varieties of harmonics about which we speculated in the preceding chapter was a matter of actual fact. Aristoxenus takes issue not only with the Pythagoreans, whose mathematical science of harmonics he finds completely irrelevant to music, but also with various more empirically minded investigators, the Harmonists, who are guilty of numerous errors—considering only some scales but not all, taking musical notation or musical instruments to reveal the nature of melody and harmonics, systematizing the tonal elements of music in a gross and uninformed way—all due in common to a proximity to practice so great as to produce a partial view or a misconception and to a failure to apply scientific principles. The Harmonists neither have a full view of the whole range of musical experience, nor do they correctly understand and analyze this experience in terms of the philosophy of science.

It is apparent then that Aristoxenus can be considered roughly as occupying a middle position between the Harmonists and the Pythagoreans, somewhat as Ptolemy does centuries later between the Aristoxenians and the Pythagoreans; but the compound represented by Aristoxenus is much more radical in nature. His epochal innovation consists in the conviction that music itself contains laws that can be determined and studied, that it can provide the basis for a science which is not mathematical or physical but peculiarly one of melody.

This is not Aristotle's conception either, which remains considerably closer to that of the Pythagoreans even though it takes the truly decisive step of breaking with Platonic metaphysics. The harmonics of Aristotle rests on arithmetic and abstracts a specifically tonal mathematics from the physical world, disregarding sonority itself but denying an independent reality to harmonic law; Aristoxenus turns to melody—a human rather than a natural manifestation and typified in the voice—and his laws are still more closely bound up in the detailed and inherent nature of his data. He has learned from Aristotle how to define the province of a science, not only how to find its natural divisions but especially how to determine the nature of its principles. This involves a kind of phenomenological awareness of a field of experience which takes on the appearance of a compact made in the interests of practicality.

Thus he refuses to be concerned, to take a characteristic instance, with the question whether melodic motion is actually physical motion, or whether the single tone, a station point in melody, is not also moving in a physical sense; to consider such problems would be to fall into a Pythagorean misconception; the science of harmonics can legitimately begin and must begin with the facts of melody. The result of Aristoxenus' application of the Aristotelian outlook is an aesthetic capable of accounting for the detailed structural properties of musical perception. In this respect it is exemplary, even if its objective attitude and its Greek interest in law and ideal form would tend to slight both individual and typical qualities of style and emotion as well as the experience of the composer and listener.

The parallel between melody and speech, originally an expression of the large unity of music, has now become a contrast as well, in reflection of the specialization of the musical sciences. It is found at the beginning of Aristoxenus' study; the intervallic motion of the voice is distinguished from the continuous motion of speech, which does not belong to the subject of harmonics; yet both are still regarded as types of melody. But intervallic motion is not the only distinguishing feature of true melody; indeed the extent to which it corresponds to law is remarkable; "although as a matter of fact there is a marvellous orderliness in the constitution of melody, music has yet been condemned, through the fault of those who have meddled with the subject, as falling into the opposite defect. The truth is that of all the objects to which the five senses apply not one other is characterized by an orderliness so extensive and so perfect." [29]

This can be seen best by comparing harmonious melody with faulty melody; both contain intervals and notes, but harmonious melody assembles these in accordance with definite principles. Even the individual tones are not points of pitch but musical functions; and two intervals may be the same in magnitude but functionally distinct. In its every feature melody involves the simultaneous cognition of permanence and change; just as we must perceive the constancy of magnitude in a transposed interval along with the change in function of its tones, so our perception of the differences of the genera depends upon the permanence of the outer tones and the changes of the inner ones.

The general nature of the laws of melodic order can be illustrated by the fundamental condition for the harmonious collocation of intervals: "Whatever be the genus, from whatever note one starts, if the melody moves in continuous progression either upwards or downwards, the fourth note in order from any note must form with it the concord of the fourth, or the fifth note in order from it the concord of the fifth. Any note that answers neither of these tests must be regarded as out of tune in relation to those notes with which it fails to form the above-mentioned concords." [30] Even though he has carefully distinguished speech from melody, Aristoxenus turns to it to illuminate the character of melodic succession.

Continuity in melody seems in its nature to correspond to that continuity in speech which is observable in the collocation of the letters. In speaking, the voice by a natural law places one letter first in each syllable, another second, another third, another fourth, and so on. This is done in no random order; rather, the growth of the whole from the parts follows a natural law. Similarly in singing, the voice seems to arrange its intervals and notes on a principle of continuity, observing a natural law of collocation, and not placing any interval at random after any other, whether equal or unequal. In inquiring after continuity we must avoid the example set by the Harmonists in their condensed diagrams, where they mark as consecutive notes those that are separated from one another by the smallest interval. For so far is the voice from being able to produce twenty-eight consecutive dieses, that it can by no effort produce three dieses in succession. If ascending after two dieses, it can produce nothing less than the complement of the fourth, and that is either eight times the smallest diesis, or falls short of it only by a minute and unmelodic interval. If descending, it cannot after the two dieses introduce any interval less than a tone. It is not, then, in the mere equality or inequality of successive intervals that we must seek the clue to the principle of continuity. We must direct our eyes to the natural laws of melody and endeavor to discover what intervals the voice is by nature capable of placing in succession in a melodic series. For if after the parhypate and the lichanos the voice can produce no note nearer than the mese, then the mese is the next note to the lichanos, whether the interval between them be twice or several times that between the lichanos and the parhypate.[31]

What human faculties are used to establish the truth of harmonic facts and laws? The criteria of judgment are a part—indeed the most crucial part—of the very conception of the science. These are foreshadowed in melody itself, with its dual aspect of constancy and change. "In making any musical phenomenon the object of scientific knowledge, its definite side should be insisted on, its indefinite features left in the background. Now in respect of the sizes of intervals and the pitch of notes, the phenomena of melody are indefinite, while in respect of functions, common qualities, and orders of arrangement, they are definite and determined." [32] The analysis of melodic perception reveals a similar dualism:

It is plain that the apprehension of a melody consists in noting with both ear and intellect every distinction as it arises in the successive sounds— successive, for melody, like all branches of music, consists in a successive production. For the apprehension of music depends on these two faculties, sense-perception and memory; for we must perceive the sound that is present, and remember that which is past. In no other way can we follow the phenomena of music.[33]

In his theory of criteria, Aristoxenus argues both against dispensing with reason and against rejecting the senses as inaccurate. He is particularly incensed over the notion that highness and lowness consist in numerical ratios and relative rates of vibration; mathematics and physics are in disagreement with melodic phenomena and completely extraneous to harmonics. The method advocated by Aristoxenus "rests in the last resort on an appeal to the two faculties of hearing and intellect":

By the former we judge the magnitudes of the intervals, by the latter we contemplate the functions of the notes. We must therefore accustom ourselves to an accurate discrimination of particulars. It is usual in geometrical constructions to use such a phrase as "Let this be a straight line"; but one must not be content with such language of assumption in the case of intervals. The geometrician makes no use of his faculty of sense-perception. He does not in any degree train his sight to discriminate the straight line, the circle, or any other figure, such training belonging rather to the practice of the carpenter, the turner, or some other such handicraftsman. But for the student of musical science accuracy of sense-perception is a fundamental requirement. For if his sense-perception is deficient, it is impossible for him to deal successfully with those questions that lie outside the sphere of sense-perception altogether.[34]

The peculiarity of the method is that hearing and reason do not really act together; they are assigned to distinct tasks. Thus reason is responsible for the logical structure of the whole science and of its particular arguments, as well as for determining the functional relationships between tones; but it does not participate in the judgment of the size of intervals; this depends solely on auditory discrimination. It is possible, then, for the infinitude of pitches comprised in the locus of any movable tone to be recognized by the intellect as discharging a single function; this infinitude will all have the same name—lichanos, say, or parhypate; indeed it is all produced on the same string, and the name of the tonal locus is properly the name of the string, but in spite of its important psychological implications Aristoxenus neglects the physical basis of the single name and the single function. He finds the functional constancy to be grounded in the nature of sensory perception; we hear every tone in the locus as an instance of the same qualitative species, and reason is consequently enabled to assign to every instance the same function; if we are led to group the pitches into a single species because they are produced on a single string of the lyre, this fact nevertheless remains outside the province of harmonics, the pertinent datum is what is given by hearing.

Underlying the spontaneous auditory grouping is the still more basic perceptual fact that dissonance is considerably more labile than consonance, a psychological distinction fully appreciated by Aristoxenus: "When we consider the magnitudes of intervals, we find that while the concords either have no locus of variation, and are definitely determined to one magnitude, or have an inappreciable locus, this definiteness is to be found in a much lesser degree in discords. For this reason, the ear is much more assured of the magnitudes of the concords than of the discords. It follows that the most accurate method of ascertaining a discord is by the principle of concordance." [35] The cooperation of hearing and intellect in establishing the functional constancy of the movable tones is as intimate a relationship as they ever display; the fundamental position of the ear remains unassailable; it can neither be invaded by reason nor reduced to mathematical or physical principles.

Almost any of the facts of harmonics will illustrate the same conception and method. Tones can be divided into halves; the fourth consists of two and a half tones; the cycle of twelve fifths returns to the original pitch: all impossible notions from the Pythagorean point of view but simple to demonstrate in Aristoxenian harmonics. Consonance may be naturally more definite than dissonance, but definite or not, the ear will hear the twelfth of a series of fifths as identical in pitch with the tone of departure, as Aristoxenus shows in demonstrating the size of the fourth. This is not because mathematical ratios can be humored by temperament; there *is* no temperament because there are no ratios; consonance is a fact given in audition, and when dissonance is measured by means of consonance, the process of measurement transpires wholly within the sphere of hearing—reason and mathematics have nothing to do with it.

Aristoxenus' conception of harmonics is easily misunderstood, but actually it testifies to the boldness of his thought and to his insight into the principles of Aristotelian science. The musical disciplines are humanistic only in the sense that they take their facts from human experience; they neither regard these facts from the vantage point of a specific method different from that of natural science, nor are they historical in orientation. As a matter of fact, music is treated very much like the natural world: it becomes an objective manifestation that is examined externally and quantitatively, its intervals subjected to division and addition in the manner of physical magnitudes; only in the irreducible psychological character of its elements and material does it remain sharply distinct from physics.

There is an interrelation of permanence and change in the rhythmical side of music also; the speed of the rhythm can change while the nature of the feet remains constant, or the nature of the feet can change while the duration of a foot remains constant, or a compound foot and a simple foot can both take up the same amount of time. "Plainly, too, unless there was a permanent quantum to deal with there could be no distinctions as to the methods of dividing it and arranging its parts. And in general, while rhythmical composition employs a rich variety of movements, the movements of the feet by which we note the rhythms are always simple and the same." [36] Again hearing and reason are called upon for rhythmical judgment. The *Rhythmics* of Aristoxenus was probably closely similar to his *Harmonics,* and equally novel and influential. It showed the same endeavor to account for the fullness of musical experience on the basis of a few principles themselves derived from this experience. The systematization is striking, although it is not arbitrary or over-elaborate, nor does it rest on a basis foreign to the aesthetic rhythms of actual music. If we realize that the perceived qualities of rhyth-mical feet—unlike those of melodic intervals—can only be described as quantitative relationships, the reliance on ratios will no longer seem to make the *Rhythmics* so Pythagorean in nature; fundamen-tally, the various feet must be regarded as given psychological facts comparable to the various intervallic successions of harmonics.

Built on the *chronos protos,* the basic unit of duration, is the *pous,* or foot, the fundamental structured element of rhythm, divided into arsis and thesis, raising and placing. The ratios 2:2, 1:2, and 2:3—called dactylic, iambic, and paeonic respectively—define the three species of rhythms, and their constituent feet exist not only in simple but in compound form with large numbers of units. The arsis and thesis of shorter feet are grasped at once by sense, but feet of longer duration must be compound, for they are readily apprehended only when they are divided into many parts. In rhythmical composition the patterns and schemes of rhythmics are applied to the material of melody and poetry and dance, achieving sensuous form. Considera-ble variety can be found, extending from rhythms that are clear and even rigid, through those whose beauty includes diversity, to those which are really not rhythms at all, since they are ugly and cannot be comprehended. Even rhythmical feet containing irrational dura-tions are recognized and have a legitimate place. The fragments testify to a science that was well founded in its method and elabo-rate in its development and that once again treated psychological facts as though they were physical data.

In his ethical views of music, Aristoxenus was closer to the out-look of Aristotle; he accepted the Platonic tradition, but with vari-ous modifications. Individual modes were of definable character and effect, but their influence was neither precise nor inescapable. On the other hand, there could be no doubt of the general moral superiority of ancient music, which was distinguished by moderation and restraint; education of the young based on music of this sort will have a lasting ethical effect, as is emphasized by one of the fragments included in the Pseudo-Plutarch *On Music:*

Now that the right molding or ruin of ingenuous manners and civil conduct lies in a well grounded musical education, Aristoxenus has made apparent. For, of those that were contemporary with him, he gives an account of Telesias the Theban, who in his youth was bred up in the noblest excellences of music, and moreover studied the works of the most famous lyrics, Pindar, Dionysius the Theban, Lamprus, Pratinas, and all the rest who were accounted most eminent; who played also to perfection upon the aulos, and was not a little industrious to furnish himself with all those other accomplishments of learning; but being past the prime of his age, he was so bewitched with the theatre's new fangles and the innovations of multiplied notes, that despising those noble precepts and that solid practice to which he had been educated, he betook himself to Philoxenus and Timotheus, and among those delighted chiefly in such as were most depraved with diversity of notes and baneful innovation. And yet, when he made it his business to make verses and labor both ways, as well in that of Pindar as that of Philoxenus, he could have no success in the latter. And the reason proceeded from the truth and exactness of his first education.[37]

The Pythagorean discipline of harmonics, more or less as it existed in the time of Aristotle's pupils, is represented by the *Section of the Canon,* a short treatise written about 300 B.C. by Euclid, the famous mathematician of Alexandria. As we mentioned in Chapter One, however, both this work and the Euclid *Elements* undoubtedly go back in large part to earlier times; Archytas is the most likely source of the *Section of the Canon,* as he is of the arithmetic and harmonic books of the *Elements* (Books VII–IX). But although Euclid may have been less of an innovator in harmonics than he was in arithmetic and geometry, his account was far from unimportant; discussed by Porphyry and Boethius, it was of considerable influence in the Middle Ages. The discipline was not restricted to the problem of the consonances; as a matter of fact, it is well represented in a general way by the discussion of the soul in the *Timaeus,* for it proceeds smoothly from consonance to the musical system. Melodic phenomena, however, which are so central in Aristoxenus, are not considered at all.

In the introductory section of the treatise, sound is traced to motion, and pitch in particular to frequency of vibration; it is not string length, simply a physical manifestation of number, that underlies tone, but vibratory motion, a specifically acoustic phenomenon. When things are compared to one another they will be subject to ratios if they are divisible into parts; in the case of sounds, then, it is fundamentally not sections of string that permit such commensuration, but the numerically divisible durations of vibration, which are connected with the successions of impulses acting on the ear. Consonant tones, nevertheless, are defined in a psychological way; they are sounds that unite and mix together, or mutually blend; consonance is the creation of a common character or a common principle. But in the Pythagorean view, the auditory manifestation is in essence numerical; accordingly Euclid postulates that the consonant sounds are in ratios that are either multiple or superparticular (2:1 or 3:2, for example), since only such ratios can be designated (in Greek) by a single word; like two consonant tones, their constituent numbers also unite in a common character!

What the introduction puts forward as the basis of harmonics, then, is that numbers may be assigned to tones, that tones may be compared by means of these numbers, and that to consonant tones there will correspond multiple and superparticular ratios. The additional axiom that the ratio 2:1 corresponds to the octave (since the octave is the closest interval to the unison) is omitted; it can be found in an alternative Pythagorean system given by Ptolemy in the first book of his *Harmonics,* but Euclid, apparently following Archytas, attempts the impossible task of deducing it as one of his theorems. Quite in accordance with the conception of Aristotle, Py-

thagorean harmonics must be regarded as a special physical department of arithmetic, a division of the theory of geometric means and
proportion with a model in the musical system. Of course the conformity of the model to the mathematics can always be called into
question, and in spite of the initial concordance, tonal properties do
not unequivocally continue to agree with the arithmetic deductions.

Starting—like the other Greek sciences of the quadrivium—with
an axiomatic but philosophically grounded congruence between
number or form and observational data (here of both a physical and
an auditory kind), the tract proceeds with a series of propositions
and their demonstrations—a mathematical form also employed by
Aristoxenus. The earlier propositions are purely arithmetical theorems dealing with ratios, or more specifically, with geometric progression, while the later propositions are concerned with the mathematical properties of tonal intervals. The proofs of the musical theorems rest not only on the preceding arithmetical propositions and
the postulates, but also on the auditory experience that the sum of
two octaves is consonant and the sum of two fifths or fourths is not,
and that the sum of a fifth and a fourth is an octave and their
difference a whole tone.

Euclid shows first that the "sum" of two equal multiple ratios will
also be a multiple ratio, and conversely, that if a multiple ratio can
be bisected, each half will also be multiple; that a superparticular
ratio does not admit either one or more mean proportionals; that the
sum of two equal nonmultiple ratios will be neither multiple nor
superparticular, and conversely, that if a nonmultiple can be bisected, each half will also be nonmultiple. He then shows, more
specifically but still without explicit reference to music, that the sum
of the ratios 3:2 and 4:3 is 2:1, that the sum of 2:1 and 3:2 is 3:1, that
the difference of 3:2 and 4:3 is 9:8, and that 9:8 taken six times is
greater than 2:1.

These arithmetic theorems dealing with the addition and division
of ratios are obviously developed because of their application to

tonal intervals, and the following theorems go on to determine the ratios that correspond to all the intervals of music, establishing the basic correspondences through conformity with auditory properties, but then deriving the ratios of the smaller intervals without appealing to particularities of perception, and simply by adding and subtracting the ratios of the consonances.

Nevertheless the claim is implicitly made that the intervals thus mathematically determined agree with our auditory perception of the musical system. The propositions in question state that the octave is multiple and the fourth and fifth superparticular; that the octave, more specifically, is duple, and the whole tone given by the ratio 9:8; that the octave is smaller than six whole tones, the fourth smaller than two and a half tones, and the fifth smaller than three and a half tones; that a whole tone cannot be divided into two or more equal parts; that successive tones of the scale can be found by adding and subtracting consonances; and that the interval bounding the *pyknon,* or closely spaced part of the scale, is never divided in half by the tone it contains, and indeed cannot be divided in half. The last two theorems, which were added to the treatise somewhat later, deal finally with the division of the canon on the basis of the ratios that have been established; they show in turn how all the fixed notes of the musical system can be measured off on such a scale and then similarly how the movable notes can be marked off.

This brief Euclidean tract thus contains our first preserved account of the complete system of Pythagorean harmonics; it treats tone as a manifestation of number, and after setting up a few fundamental correspondences between arithmetical properties and perceived intervallic attributes, it develops the entire tonal system in conformity with mathematical structure, paying no attention at all to actual works of art and to the individual and public features of their melodic language, whether as natural products or as cultural ones.

It was not only Aristoxenus who took issue with the musical

conceptions of the Pythagoreans; complementing his harmonic theories and giving them additional depth and a broader foundation is the important musical philosophy of Theophrastus, Aristotle's successor and most influential disciple. An extensive fragment of his *On Music*, found in Porphyry's *Commentary on Ptolemy's Harmonics*,[38] examines the nature of music in detail.

Melodic motion, as it is expressed in the voice, acts upon the soul in accordance with the intention of the singer; this motion thus becomes a motion of the soul, restoring it to calm by eliminating the disturbances of the passions. But although the effect of the voice is definite, the attempt to deduce it from the mathematical relationships of the intervals is a mistake. Quantity is not the basis of melodic differences nor the principle of music, even though such a conception may seem superior to the view of the Harmonists, who rely only on hearing for musical judgment. If melodic differences were quantitative, they would have to derive from differences in magnitude throughout a melody and not only in the case of individual consonances, so that even the varied shades of the genera would be distinguished by the magnitude of the intervals, a consequence Theophrastus evidently feels to be quite improbable. Nothing less is implied by the thesis that melodic inflections rest on number, or that interval and melody actually are number.

Also if tones consist of nothing beyond the relationships of number, then every group of things standing in particular numerical relationships to one another must constitute a melody. The true state of affairs, however, can be seen in the instance of color, which possesses quantity in addition to its essential nature; similarly a tone is one thing and its quantity something quite different. This means that we are dealing with more than pure audibility, and the alternative arises that lower and higher are distinguished from one another either simply as tones or in reference to quantity. Now if quantity is the basis, the specific nature of the voice could consist in nothing other than this, for it can always be apprehended either as high or low; each vocal tone is higher or lower in relation to some other, so that the quantity of the one is numerically greater and that of the other smaller. If we then eliminate number, nothing will remain as a basis for the nature of the voice; since one tone is always higher or lower than another, the voice must have quantity or it will not be a voice.

But if higher and lower tones are distinguished from one another simply as tones, Theophrastus continues, we are able to forego quantity altogether, for the natural difference of the tones will be perceptible and will also be sufficient to produce a melody. Tonal differences will then be like distinctions in color, and will rest not on magnitude but on qualitative peculiarity. If we mix equal amounts of white and black we cannot say that the number of the white exceeds or is less than that of the black; and the same is true of sweet and sour, for each of these is the same in quality no matter how far it extends.

Theophrastus does recognize special laws of quantity in tone, but the discussion of these, based as it is on a sensitive but qualitative science, constitutes a section of his inquiry that is quite difficult to comprehend. The numbers the Pythagoreans find in pitch are considered to be the tonal analogue of spatial quantity in other sensory modes, but irrelevant to pitch itself. High and low tones are not composed of a multitude of constituents, nor do they rest on larger or smaller numbers; their quantitative measure follows other principles. Singers, for example, need a certain amount of power both for high and for low tones, although the power is directed in opposite ways in the two instances; similarly, power is demanded both by narrow auloi and by wide ones (the pitch remaining the same, however, in this illustration).

A single aulos reveals a contrasting principle; less force is required for high tones than for low, the determining factor now being the relative distances of the holes from the mouthpiece. In the case of strings, the lower ones are thicker to the same degree that the thin ones are more tense; thus the tones of thick strings are heavier to the extent that the tones of thinner ones are more penetrating; the larger and more diffused sound comes from the larger source.

The argument is extended to consonance. How can certain tones concord with one another, Theophrastus asks, if they do not have something in common? More and less do not permit any fusion, since what is excessive will obviously protrude; consequently that which is more penetrating must be paired with a larger amount of that which is less penetrating in order for balance to be achieved; in consonance there must be an equality of the components. If the higher tone involved a higher number, there would be no consonance; if it had some larger measurement not matched by the other tone that was responsible for its audibility at a greater distance, it would never be able to form a concord, whether it reached the ear alone or together with the lower tone. In short, consonance presupposes some agreement between the tones; a balance of force must exist even though the force of each tone has its own peculiar form. Actually the specific property of high tones is an inherent distinctness rather than a penetration; they are perceived further than low tones in the same way that white is as compared to another color; they are recognized not because they depend on different numbers, but attract our attention in greater degree as a result of a fundamental difference in nature. Thus while low tones are widely diffused, we hear high ones more readily because of their specific property and not because of any numerical quantity they contain. Even if they penetrated further, they would not be higher because they depended upon larger numbers but because of the character of their motion: high sounds move more directly forward and upward, and low ones more equally in all directions.

Theophrastus seeks to substantiate this difference by appealing in turn to wind instruments, to singing, and to string instruments; in each case the low tones spread out more and the high ones are more directional. But if low tones spread out symmetrically to the same

The Peripatetics

extent that high ones penetrate forwards, he argues, they will not involve smaller numbers; indeed we can see in auloi that a large instrument is low in sound because its air column is larger. And by no means are high tones distinguished by a greater velocity, for they would then reach the ear earlier and no fusion would ensue; consonance requires that both tones travel with the same velocity. Thus the relationships of tones can in no way be attributed to differences in numbers.

Nor can intervals be considered the cause or principle of tonal differences; we might just as well consider ekmelic (unmelodic) tones to be the cause of emmelic (melodic) ones. Now there could be no emmelic tones if the existence of ekmelic ones was inconceivable; similarly there could be no particular field of knowledge if we were not able to imagine the lack of this knowledge. But the lack of knowledge is not an actuality that causes the knowledge, nor is it in any sense an obstruction; instead the lack is a necessary presupposition that makes the presence possible. Thus intervals also are not the cause of melody in the sense that they produce it, but can only be said not to obstruct it, and, more positively, to permit it.

Again, if we sing all the possible intermediate tones between those of a melodic progression we will produce innumerable ekmelic ones, and these would have to exist even if we did not sing or consciously presuppose them; they must be absent in order for emmelic tones to manifest themselves, but we cannot for that reason call them an obstruction. Theophrastus is far from clear, but what he argues is that intervals, like ekmelic tones, are a precondition for the manifestation of specifically tonal differences and melody. Neither intervals nor ekmelic tones are in fact sonorous, but since the distinctions of tonal quality that constitute melody necessarily appear at certain intervals and only by virtue of the circumstance that other tones do not appear, the existence of melody depends upon intervals even if it is not constituted by them. In sum, then, neither numbers nor intervals are the basis of melody, but only the inherent qualitative differences between tones; in the case of consonance, these differences are accompanied by a balance of specific quantitative factors.

In addition to its positive value, Theophrastus' discussion comprises a detailed polemic against Heraclides Ponticus, the pupil of Plato, and Archytas, since both of these philosophers expounded the Pythagorean view that the essence of sound was to be found in physical vibration. The related belief, held by both Plato and Aristotle, that high sounds had a higher velocity of transmission than lower ones, is also subjected to criticism. Common to the theories of vibration and velocity is the explanation of pitch as basically numerical, and in taking issue with this conception, Theophrastus joined Aristoxenus in a rejection of Pythagoreanism that is much more radical than that of their teacher, for in spite of his revision of the status of number, Aristotle made use of it in his own way to account for the phenomena of music.

Nevertheless, the phenomenological position of Theophrastus and Aristoxenus is a logical development not only of Aristotle's philosophy of science but of his general metaphysical outlook. This can be seen in the fragmentary *Metaphysics* of Theophrastus, which extends Aristotle's refusal to grant independent reality to form and number into a general disinclination to seek the explanation of phenomena outside the specific nature of the objects that manifest them. The thought of Theophrastus is characterized by a kind of philosophic principle of parsimony. His point of departure, however, is still the dualism of reason and sense; these have separate objects—eternal and perishable respectively—and the basic problem of metaphysics is to determine the connection between the two. "If the objects of reason are found in mathematical objects only, as some say, neither is their connection with objects of sense very conspicuous, nor do they appear, in general, equal to their whole task; for they seem to have been, as it were, devised by us in the act of investing things with figures and shapes and ratios, and to have no nature in and of themselves; and if this is not so, at least they seem not to connect with the things of nature in such a way as to produce in them, as it were, life and motion; for not even number itself does so, which some in fact rank as the first and most dominant of all things." [39]

In his search for the true objects of reason, Theophrastus rejects one possibility after another, incorporating each in turn into the objects of sense; ultimately he is led to doubt even the teleological principle of a divine and nonquantitative final cause. His examination of number uncovers the crucial issue of idealism, which determines equally the musical conception of Aristotle and the very different one of his pupils; if numbers are independent objects of reason, their connection with objects of sense becomes problematical and they are powerless to explain perceived properties and qualities. This strikes at the heart of any Pythagorean philosophy of sensible music.

The *Metaphysics* makes it clear, however, that even if harmony and order have no independent reality, they are still important characteristics of inanimate and animate nature. The motions of the universe proceed in harmony; the whole is concordant with itself to the greatest extent possible, and well harmonized "as though it were a city or an animal." [40] Order and definiteness are equally characteristic of the arts, since they imitate nature, and of the sciences as well.

In this connection Theophrastus groups together grammar, music, and the mathematical disciplines, a list which is interesting because it brings both lower and higher studies under the head of order instead of distinguishing them from one another because of their different ethical import. This permits music to appear alongside grammar and still possess a scientific character, while its implied absence from the mathematical disciplines is in accordance with Peripatetic views after Aristotle. Rhetoric and logic have not yet appeared among the earlier studies, nor has music been rejected; the whole series provides us with a valuable glimpse of an intermediate stage in the development of the liberal arts.

The important point about Theophrastus' conception of harmony, however, is that all the varied harmonic manifestations are not representatives of a separate and eternal entity; thus they do not have an inherent identity or even a detailed correspondence of a musical kind; each is to be investigated in its own right. This follows from the basic tenets of Peripatetic philosophy, and with the important exception of the early and more distinctly Platonic phase of Aristotle's thought, it can be taken as generally true of Aristotle and Aristoxenus as well as Theophrastus. As a result, Peripatetic conceptions of harmony—although not of harmonics—are no longer an integral part of the philosophy of music.

If the true center of musical thought becomes the scientific and aesthetic analysis of the inherent properties of sensible music, the traditional notions of ethical effect and social influence continue to be endorsed also, even though they are generalized into a variety of purely emotional characteristics. We have seen that the large fragment of Theophrastus' *On Music* included in Porphyry's *Commentary* regards music as producing a movement of the soul that frees it from the passions, and scattered references to Theophrastus [41] in Censorinus, Plutarch, Athenaeus, Pliny, and Aulus Gellius not only confirm and extend this conception, but also show that he subscribed to a surprising variety of musical effects. Music frees the soul from feelings of pain and pleasure and desire; the sensory impression it produces is of great strength because hearing is a sense of unusual susceptibility; it is even able to cure disease, aulos playing in particular being a remedy for the poisonous bite of the viper. These influences of music on the individual have their complement in the social values upon which Aristoxenus insists.

That Theophrastus also concerned himself with the basis of music in human nature can be seen from a discussion in the *Ars gramma-*

tica of Marius Victorinus; [42] indeed in his *On Music,* Theophrastus was very probably the originator of a comprehensive aesthetic theory built on a natural or biological foundation. The elements of such a theory had existed for some time. In the *Laws,* Plato had emphasized the sense for harmonic and rhythmic expression, but in connection with Pythagorean concepts of harmony and number, such a sense seemed given to man by the gods. This was an active concept of aesthetics, nevertheless; and underlying the sense for order was a truly innate and spontaneous tendency to vocal expression and bodily movement, which appeared in earliest infancy.

But to work such notions up into a developed theory was a considerable undertaking. The task was made possible by an anthropology which conceived man as a member of a series extending from natural substances to plants and animals. Human reason still preserves a divine character in Aristotle, although its status has become equivocal; but fundamentally, the biological naturalism of Peripatetic thought eliminated the sharp duality of body and mind, and permitted soul and reason to become the formal determinants of man's essential substance; man was then distinctive and yet a continuous and coherent part of the world. Virtue and thought could become part of his natural endowment, and the higher values of ethics and aesthetics were not separated by a chasm from the more primitive and irrational human expressions and desires. The outlook is clearly revealed in Aristotle's *Politics,* primarily with respect to speech and society:

Now, that man is more of a political animal than bees or any other gregarious animals is evident. Nature, as we often say, makes nothing in vain, and man is the only animal whom she has endowed with the gift of speech. And whereas mere voice is but an indication of pleasure or pain, and is therefore found in other animals (for their nature attains to the perception of pleasure and pain and the intimation of them to one another, and no further), the power of speech is intended to set forth the expedient and inexpedient, and therefore likewise the just and the unjust. And it is a characteristic of man that he alone has any sense of good and evil, of just and unjust, and the like, and the association of living beings who have this sense makes a family and a state.[43]

Similarly, Theophrastus not only grounds all the goods and values of ethics in human nature, but finds in addition that aesthetic perception and the sense for harmony and rhythm need not look elsewhere for their explanation. They are manifestations that may be known directly, and belong to the original and innate principles of man. But music not only rests on natural disposition; it requires an elaboration of this foundation; to the spontaneous and natural there must be added a detailed formulation and manipulation. The development of musical endowment takes place through the emotions, through pleasure, enthusiasm, and grief or anger. In the unformed expression of musical impulses, however, there is already contained a natural kind of pleasure, and aesthesis, too, is joined to feeling, as Theophrastus holds in his *On the Senses*.[44] Pleasure and pain alike arise from sense perception, but since this is in accord with nature it is linked more intimately with pleasure than with pain; only if the intensity of the stimulation does not suitably correspond to the organ of sense does the pleasure disappear.

In his *Poetics,* Aristotle also had connected pleasure with the exercise of natural functions and even with art; it attached to learning and for this reason also to imitation and thus to art as well. But in deriving music itself from native capacity plus emotional life, Theophrastus set up a very different and active theory of aesthetics, the loss of which must be considered a great misfortune. What we know of it explains quite readily why his view of music grew out of the voice and its natural tendencies, and indeed his productive aesthetics is only the culmination of the general concern in antiquity with an active rather than a passive view of art, and this in turn is doubtless due to the dominant position of music as contrasted with the greater influence of painting on modern aesthetic thought.

In any event, the Peripatetic theories of musical expression and of a science based on the voice and directed towards harmonic and rhythmic composition complete the Greek conception of music, adding a concern with creative origins to an earlier interest in musical influences and the metaphysical status of the work of art itself, or turning it, we might say, from philosophy to aesthetics. At the same time music was increasingly humanized; closely connected with the external world, even its ethical properties had rested in part on a harmonic and mathematical nature; but treated as a natural vocal expression formed by feeling, it lost its cosmic import and cast aside mathematical and physical laws to find its own inherent principles. These could be called harmonic only by an extension of the term.

Notes

I. Conceptions of Harmony

1. Frg. 6. The passage in question can be found in Diels and Kranz, I, 409. There are brief but valuable discussions of the controversy over the authenticity of the Philolaic fragments in Burnet, *Early Greek Philosophy*, pp. 279–84, and in Kirk and Raven, pp. 308–13. Burnet regards the fragments as suspicious; Kirk and Raven conclude, more definitely, that they are a skillful forgery based on Aristotle.

2. See Meyer. The "Wortindex" of Diels and Kranz contains a useful, compact guide to the occurrence of the word in pre-Socratic philosophy (III, 72).

3. See the excellent study by Kahn.

4. The literature on early Pythagoreanism is vast; its extent corresponds to the importance of the subject, but is hardly justified by the amount of dependable information available. Reliance on Neo-Pythagorean sources is dangerous, recourse to Plato's *Timaeus* less so. Aristotle is concerned with the later Pythagorean mathematicians rather than with the original sect. Works of particular value are Delatte's *Etudes,* and B. L. van der Waerden. Representative accounts of Pythagoras and his school are those in Burnet, ch. 2, and in Heath, *Greek Mathematics,* vol. I, chs. 3, 5. On ancient mathematics in general and the question of the originality of the Pythagoreans see Neugebauer.

5. The evidence is marshaled in Cornford, *Plato and Parmenides,* ch. 1.

6. There are recent detailed studies of Heraclitus by Kirk and by Wheelwright. The fragments can also be found in Burnet, ch. 3; in Diels and Kranz, vol. I, ch. 22; and in Kirk and Raven, ch. 6. So many of them come into question here that there is little point in singling any out for mention.

7. *Symposium* 187a–b.

8. See Cornford; Burnet, ch. 4; Diels and Kranz, vol. I, ch. 28; and Kirk and Raven, ch. 10.

9. Burnet, ch. 5; Diels and Kranz, vol. I, ch. 31; Kirk and Raven, ch. 14. See especially frgs. 6, 8, 9, 11, 12, 17, 20, 21, 22, 23, 35, 36, 71, 98, 107.

10. Burnet, ch. 6; Diels and Kranz, vol. II, ch. 59; Kirk and Raven, ch. 15. See especially frgs. 12 and 17.

11. *Introduction to Arithmetic* II.26.

12. Diels and Kranz, vol. I, ch. 44; see note 1 above. There is a good account of the Philolaic cosmology in Dreyer, ch. 2.

13. See Burnet, pp. 99–100; Diels and Kranz, vol. I, ch. 45; and Kirk and Raven, pp. 313–17.

14. See Diels and Kranz, vol. I, ch. 47, and Heath, I, 11, 14, 85–86, 90, 212–16, 246–49.

15. *De architectura* I.i.16.

16. *Theaetetus* 145a–d.

17. *Protagoras* 318d–e.

18. *Lesser Hippias* 363b–368.

19. *Cratylus* 404e–406a.

20. *Symposium* 186–88.

21. *Republic* 614b–621. See the discussion of this passage in James Adam's edition (Cambridge, 1902) and in the Introduction by A. Diès to the Budé edition (Paris, 1947). Boyancé has also dealt instructively with the myth in *Le culte des Muses* and in "Les Muses et l'harmonie des sphères," *Mélanges Félix Grat*.

22. Since countless philosophical, theological, and mathematical works are commentaries on the *Timaeus* in fact but not in name, the total volume of writing based on this dialogue is incredibly large. Older commentaries are of interest as documents that express the musical thought of their time; recent commentaries serve as the immediate background of our own analysis. The most valuable scholarly commentaries of the nineteenth and twentieth centuries are Boeckh (first published in the early years of the nineteenth century); T. Martin; Stallbaum; Shorey; Rivaud, "Notice," in his *Timée* (Paris, 1925), vol. X of the Budé edition of Plato, and in "Études platoniciennes," *Revue d'histoire de la philosophie;* Taylor; and Cornford, *Plato's Cosmology*. The musical details of the structure of the soul were restudied recently by Handschin in "The 'Timaeus' Scale," *Musica Disciplina*. The most debated passages of the *Timaeus* have been precisely those that deal with harmony, and in particular with the creation of the soul; but while some of the details are problematical, they are also unimportant, and do not affect the general import of Plato's discussion. More serious is the question of the nature of his concepts, of the correct balance of literal and figurative significance in the notions of the

Artificer, the materials of the soul, creation in time, and so forth. Each age and each exegete has given different relative weight to the components of poetry and philosophy, but this peculiarly Platonic compound has its own unique eloquence and meaning, and is best left undisturbed.

23. *Laws* 967e. The translations of Plato are by Jowett.

24. *Timaeus* 69b.

25. *Philebus* 26b–c.

26. See Burnet, pp. 193–96; Diels and Kranz, vol. I, ch. 24; and Kirk and Raven, ch. 8.

27. Frgs. 20, 21, 23, 26.

28. Frg. 17.

29. The works of the Hippocratic corpus that are important for our purpose can be found in vols. I, II, and IV of Loeb Classical Library edition.

30. Armand Delatte, "Les harmonies dans l'embryologie hippocratique," *Mélanges Paul Thomas*.

31. See note 20 above.

32. *Phaedo* 85e–86d. It is a considerable step from Alcmaeon's concept of bodily health as an *isonomia* of pairs of opposed qualities to Simmias' concept of the soul as a *harmonia* of the body; for one thing, the simple balance of equals must be supplanted by the proportions of harmonic theory. Yet in his account, Simmias clearly leans on medical theory, and it is quite possible that the influence of Alcmaeon or of Hippocratic medicine on Pythagorean thought is responsible for his views. Medicine could logically bring about a materialistic transformation of religious ideas.

33. *Phaedo* 91c–95a.

34. *Republic* 439–44.

35. *Ibid.*, 443d–e.

36. *Ibid.*, 410b–412a.

37. *Timaeus* 41c–42a, 69c–72d.

38. See note 35 above.

39. *Republic* 441d–443.

40. *Phaedrus* 256b.

41. *Lysis* 214c–d.

42. *Republic* 432a.

43. *Phaedo* 92c.

44. *Gorgias* 482b–c.

45. *Laches* 188c–e, 193d–e.

46. *Republic* 486. Ideas of harmony often emphasize pleasure and neglect structure. The underlying conception can be that of a mean value itself as a harmony; thus a harmonious voice is one that has a well-chosen intermediate nature in respect of pitch and loudness, although it can also be one that is simply pleasant in quality. In such qualitative conceptions of harmony, which proliferate endlessly, there are generally some vague implications either of mean values or of compatible constituents, but the mathematical structure is really of no importance and cannot be specified.

47. *Philebus* 16c–17.

48. *Republic* 531a–c.

49. *Symposium* 215b–216a.

50. *Phaedo* 84e–85c.

51. *Ibid.*, 60d–61a.

52. *Phaedrus* 258e–259.

II. Theories of Musical Ethics

1. *Odyssey* XIX.457.

2. A great deal of information about the Dionysiac, Orphic, and Pythagorean cults is assembled in the classic work of Rohde, chs. 8–11. See also Harrison, *Prolegomena,* and Guthrie, *Orpheus.*

3. *Laws* 790e–791a. Plato actually describes the cure of Bacchic frenzy as an allopathic process; music produces a quietness of the soul not by aggravating and then discharging an evil affection, but by combating and overcoming it with an opposed and beneficial external motion. Yet the process is thought of as cathartic.

4. *Ion* 533e–534a.

5. Evidence may be found in the remarks Aristotle makes on the Phrygian mode (*Politics* 1340b.4–5) and the aulos (*ibid.*, 1342b.2–7).

6. Herodotus *The Persian Wars* II.81.

7. *Ibid.*

8. See, for example, *Metaphysics* 985b.24.

9. *Odyssey* XII.39–45.

10. *Politics* 1341b.

11. *Sophist* 231b. In *Laws* 790c–792, after describing the musical cure of Bacchic frenzy, Plato proceeds to apply the theory of this process to education, seeking to avoid occasions of sorrow and fear altogether, as well as to strengthen the habits of cheerfulness and courage.

12. *Meno* 80a.

13. *Republic* 399c–d.

14. *Symposium* 215b–216b.

15. See, for example, the interesting study by Georgiades, *Der griechische Rhythmus,* or the reworked English version, *Greek Music.*

16. *Timaeus* 80a–b. Because instrumental music lacks imitative power, it readily becomes either dedication to pleasure as opposed to good, or a manifestation of harmony, which makes it morally significant and at the same time a sensuous approximation of scientific knowledge. This point is discussed below.

17. Important recent histories of ancient education are Jaeger's *Paideia;* Marrou's *A History of Education in Antiquity;* and Lasserre, "L'éducation musicale dans la grèce antique," in his edition of Pseudo-Plutarch.

18. *Republic* 410c–412b.

19. *Symposium* 176e. See also *Protagoras* 347, where the entertainment furnished by girls who dance and play the aulos and lyre is similarly set aside in favor of discourse.

20. *Laws* 700–701c provides a picture of the moral decay of music and its repercussions in the early part of the fourth century. See also *Republic* 700a–b.

21. Aristophanes, *Five Comedies,* p. 272.

22. *Ibid.,* p. 273.

23. *Ibid.,* p. 287.

24. *Ibid.,* pp. 287–88.

25. This can be seen clearly in the intransigent and rebellious views defended by Callicles in Plato's *Gorgias* 482c–484c.

26. See the discussion in Georgiades.

27. As an imitator alone, the artist has little claim to respect; if he really understood the objects he imitated, he would devote himself to them and not to art. See *Republic* 597d–602c.

28. Even though issue can be taken with it in some respects, Abert's study of the ethical character of the various constituents of Greek music, *Die Lehre vom Ethos,* is still a basic and definitive collection of the evidence, most of it unfortunately from post-classical sources.

29. See Buecheler; "Damon," in *Paulys Real-Encyclopädie; Ryffel,* "Eukosmia," *Museum Helviticum;* and Lasserre's edition of Pseudo-Plutarch, pp. 53–79.

30. *Crito* 50d.

31. *Protagoras* 325c–326.

32. *Republic* 394e–398b, 401.

33. Even here, however, we have seen that he regards the musical cures as allopathic (see note 3 above).

34. The emotional evils of poetry are discussed at length as part of the thoroughgoing condemnation of imitative art in the *Republic*, Book X.

35. *Republic* 401d–402a.

36. This is actually the prevailing view both in the *Republic* and in the *Laws*.

37. *Republic* 520e–540.

38. See ch. 1, p. 19.

39. *Republic* 546d–547a.

40. The discussion of music in the *Laws* is found largely in Books II and VII.

41. *Republic* 408d–409.

42. For a comprehensive discussion of the evidence that bears on the nature of the *nomos,* see Greiser.

43. *Laws* 700–701c.

44. *Ibid.,* 795e–796b.

45. *Ibid.,* 788–98, 809b–812a.

III. The Philosophy and Aesthetics of Music

1. *Laches* 188d.

2. Hermann Koller, "Enkyklios Paideia," *Glotta.*

3. *Theaetetus* 172b–176a. "Such are the two characters, Theodorus," says Socrates at the conclusion of this digression, "the one of the freeman, who has been trained in liberty and leisure, whom you call the philosopher—him we cannot blame because he appears simple and of no account when he has to perform some menial task, such as packing up bed-clothes, or flavoring a sauce or fawning speech; the other character is that of the man who is able to do all this kind of service smartly and neatly, but knows not how to wear his cloak like a gentleman; still less with the music of discourse can he hymn the true life aright which is lived by immortals or men blessed of heaven."

4. *Metaphysics* 997a–998a; *Physics* 193b–194b; *Posterior Analytics* 76a, 78b–79a.

5. *Cratylus* 421e–426b.

6. *Philebus* 16b–18d.

7. *Theaetetus* 202e–208b.

8. Hermann Koller, "Stoicheion," *Glotta.*

9. *Statesman* 284a.

10. *Philebus* 26a.

11. *Gorgias* 503–4.

12. *Philebus* 55c–56c.

13. *Critias* 107. See also the passage of *Theaetetus* cited in note 7 above.

14. *Ibid.,* 108c.

15. *Eryxias* 403c–d.

16. *Symposium* 187c–e.

17. Thus the musical scale of the *Timaeus*—nonsensible and extending beyond the range of musical practice—is the basic pattern both of the soul and of music. Realizing it in sound as it is given produces the Dorian musical ideal, capable of preserving or restoring temperance and order to the soul. Placing it at different positions, or tensions, produces all the variety of the Greek scales, which are capable in turn of arousing all the corresponding affective states of the soul, each consisting of an analogous aspect or displacement of the underlying psychic structure, and each brought to life by appropriate rhythmic patterns. Here is the key, then, that simultaneously explains musical and ethical theory. In connection with the scales, see Lohmann—a derivation, somewhat forced and overly symmetrical, of the whole system of Greek music from etymological evidence and general philosophic considerations. The word *tonos* means "tension," "whole-tone," and "scale," meanings still present in the English *tone,* and Greek music reveals the interesting interconnection of all three senses of the word, for the scales (*tonoi*) were not only different tensions of the basic ideal pattern, but each was characterized and defined in its particular tension by the position of the distinctive interval of the whole-tone (between the notes *mese* and *paramese*), the single interval that remained unchanged throughout the various genera and shades of the scales.

18. *Ion.*

IV. The Peripatetics

1. *Menexenus* 235e–236a.

2. See Grenfell and Hunt, *The Hibeh Papyri,* Vol. I, No. 13; Abert, "Ein neuer musikalische Papyrusfund," *Zeitschrift;* Ruelle, "Le papyrus musical d'Hibeh," *Revue de philologie;* Crönert, "Die Hibehrede uber die

Musik," *Hermes;* and Janssens, "De muziekaesthetische papyrus van
Hibeh," *Philologische Studien.*

3. Diogenes Laertius VI.27, 73.

4. Diels and Kranz, vol. II, ch. 68; Kirk and Raven, ch. 17.

5. Aristoxenus, *Harmonics,* p. 188 (Macran edition).

6. *Metaphysics* I.9; III passim; VII.8,13,14; XIII; XIV. The only exception to Aristotle's negative position with regard to the independent existence of an ideal harmony is the fragment found in the Pseudo-Plutarch *On Music* 23–25 (Lasserre translation); the chief ideas are contained in the following passages: "Harmony is divine, participating in the nature of the gods and in the nature of beauty and of every excellence. . . . Also, it has a structure entirely comparable to that of nature, participating, with its parts, in the essence of the even, the odd, and the even-odd. . . . Finally, as to the sensations that harmony creates in the body, those that are celestial and divine because they bring understanding to man thanks to the aid of a god—namely vision and hearing—manifest harmony by sound and by light; but the other sensations, which assist these two, also owe their existence to harmony, for they are not able to discharge any of their functions without harmony, and if they are less important than vision and hearing, they are not different in essence. But it is vision and hearing that most logically lay claim to power and beauty, because in entering the body they impress upon it the presence of a god." This fragment is introduced in the Pseudo-Plutarch dialogue in connection with a discussion of the *Timaeus,* and the work of Aristotle from which it is taken may very well be of similar nature. The use of the terms "boundless" and "limited" in the description of the structure of harmony (which is here specifically taken to be the ratios given by the tetractys and comprised in the series 12, 9, 8, 6) implies a Pythagorean identification of numbers with things; the fundamental constituents of the cosmos are identical with the bases of number, just as they are in the Philolaic fragment 6. As we have seen (Chapter 1, note 1), the Philolaic fragments may postdate Aristotle; Xenocrates was an adherent of the Pythagorean theory they contain. On the other hand, the theory itself is undoubtedly an old one; it is consonant with all the evidence we possess of earlier Pythagorean views, and the creation of the soul in the *Timaeus,* to say nothing of the whole structure of the material world, falls into place perfectly as an elaboration and refinement of Pythagorean ideas of this type. It is clear,

in any event, that the work from which the Pseudo-Plutarch fragment is taken must date from the time Aristotle was still a representative of Platonism; indeed he is often regarded as such in late antiquity, and the Platonic elements of his thought—which really never disappear even in his later writings—did in fact facilitate the philosophic syncretism that grew up during the centuries after his death.

7. *On the Heavens* II.8–9.

8. See *On the Soul* I, which is devoted almost exclusively to a polemic against previous theories (the refutation of the harmonic theory is found in I.4), and for the relevant *Eudemus* fragments, see vol. XII (*Select Fragments*) of Aristotle, *Works,* ed. by Ross, pp. 19–22.

9. *On the Soul* 426a.27–29.

10. *Ibid.,* 426a.27–426b.8

11. *Physics* I.5.

12. *On the Heavens* III–IV; *Meteorology* IV.1; *On Generation and Corruption* II.1–8.

13. *On the Soul* 407b.28–408a.28; *Physics* 246b.4–19.

14. *Nicomachean Ethics* 1106a.14–1107a.27; 1131a.10–1134a.16; 1138b. 18–1139a.17; 1173a.15–28.

15. *Poetics* 1–6.

16. *Politics* VIII. See also Busse, "Musikästhetik," *Rheinisches Museum;* Vetter, "Die antike Musik," *Archiv für Musikforschung;* and E. Koller.

17. This point is persuasively developed in E. Koller, where it is argued that *diagoge* cannot be abstracted from the social context of the ideal polis as envisaged in Plato's *Laws.*

18. *Phaedrus* 237a–b. "Come, O ye Muses, melodious, as ye are called, whether you have received this name from the character of your strains, or because the Melians are a musical race, help, O help me in the tale which my good friend here desires me to rehearse, in order that his friend whom he always deemed wise may seem to him to be wiser than ever."

19. *Laws* 722d–e.

20. *Rhetoric* 1403b.26–35.

21. *Politics* 1340b.17–19.

22. See note 6 above.

23. *Politics* 1340a.24.

24. *Ibid.,* 1340a.22.

25. *On the Soul* 420b.1–420b.4. For a discussion of the actuality of sound see 425b.26–426a.26, and for the notion of the mean as a harmony see notes 9 and 10 above.

26. *Generation of Animals* V.7.

27. *Ibid.*

28. *Topics* I.15.

29. Aristoxenus, *Harmonics*, p. 168.

30. *Ibid.*, p. 205.

31. *Ibid.*, pp. 184–85.

32. *Ibid.*, p. 217.

33. *Ibid.*, pp. 193–94.

34. *Ibid.*, p. 189.

35. *Ibid.*, p. 206.

36. *Ibid.*, p. 190.

37. *On Music* 31. For available editions see "Pseudo–Plutarch" in the Bibliography; the translation of the passage cited is by John Philips, and can be found in Plutarch's *Miscellanies and Essays*, I, 125.

38. See Ingemar Düring, "Ptolemaios und Porphyrios über die Musik," *Göteborgs Högskolas Arsskrift 40*, p. 161ff.

39. Theophrastus, *Metaphysics*, pp. 3–4.

40. *Ibid.*, p. 16.

41. See "Theophrast," in *Paulys Real-Encyclopädie.*

42. See Dirlmeier, "Die Oikeiosis-Lehre Theophrasts," *Philologus Supplementband*, pp. 98–100.

43. *Politics* 1253a.7–1253a.18.

44. *On the Senses* 32–33; see the edition by Stratton, pp. 94–95.

Bibliography

Abert, H. "Antike," Handbuch der Musikgeschichte. Edited by G. Adler. 2d ed. Berlin, 1930.

—— "Antike Musikerlegenden," Festschrift Rochus von Liliencron. Leipzig, 1910.

—— "Bericht über die Literatur zur griechischen Musik aus den Jahren 1903–1908," Jahresbericht der klassischen Altertumswissenschaft 144, 1909.

—— "Bericht über die Literatur zur griechischen Musik aus den Jahren 1909–1921," Jahresbericht der klassischen Altertumswissenschaft 193, 1922.

—— "Der gegenwärtige Stand der Forschung über die antike Musik," Jahrbuch der Musikbibliothek Peters für 1921. Part II: Festgabe Max Friedlaender.

—— Die Lehre vom Ethos in der griechischen Musik. Leipzig, 1899.

—— "Die Musik der Griechen," in his Gesammelte Schriften und Vorträge. Halle, 1929.

—— "Der neue Aristoxenosfund von Oxyrhynchos," Sammelbände der internationalen Musikgesellschaft 1, 1899–1900.

—— "Ein neuer musikalische Papyrusfund," Zeitschrift der internationalen Musikgesellschaft 8, 1906.

—— "Die Stellung der Musik in der antiken Kultur," Antike 2, 1926.

Ahlvers, A. Zahl und Klang bei Platon. Bern, 1952.

Ambros, A. W. Geschichte der Musik. Vol. I. Breslau, 1862.

Anderson, W. D. "The Importance of Damonian Theory in Plato's Thought," Transactions of the American Philological Association 86, 1955.

Anticlo, G. R. "Gli spiriti della musica nella tragedia greca," Rivista musicale italiana 20, 1913.

Archer-Hind, R. D. The Timaeus of Plato. London, 1888.

Aristides Quintilianus. De musica. Edited by A. Jahn. Berlin, 1882.

—— Von der Musik. Translated by R. Schäfke. Berlin, 1937.

Aristophanes. Five Comedies. Cleveland, 1948.

—— Works. Edited by B. B. Rogers. 3 vols. London, 1924–1927. Loeb Classical Library.

Aristotle. Dialogorum Fragmenta. Edited by R. Walzer. Florence, 1934.
—— Fragmenta. Edited by V. Rose. Leipzig, 1886.
—— Opera. Edited by the Academia Regia Borussica. 5 vols. Berlin, 1831–1870.
—— Les problèmes. Translated by J. Barthélémy-Saint-Hilaire. 2 vols. Paris, 1891.
—— Les problèmes musicaux. Edited by F. A. Gevaert and J. C. Vollgraff. 3 vols. Gent, 1899–1902.
—— Works. 22 vols. London, 1926–1962. Loeb Classical Library.
—— The Works. Edited by W. D. Ross and others. 12 vols. Oxford, 1908–1952.
Aristoxenus. L'armonica. Translated by R. da Rios. Rome, 1954.
—— Elementa harmonica. Edited by R. da Rios. Rome, 1954.
—— The Harmonics. Edited by H. S. Macran. Oxford, 1902.
—— Die harmonischen Fragmente. Edited by P. Marquard. Berlin, 1868.
—— Melik und Rhythmik des classischen Hellenenthums. Edited by R. Westphal. 2 vols. Leipzig, 1883–1893.
—— Rhythmica. Edited by G. P. Pighi. Bologna, 1959.
Arteaga, E. Lettere musico-filologiche; Del ritmo sonoro e del ritmo muto nella musica degli antichi. Madrid, 1944.
Ast, F. Lexicon Platonicum. 3 vols. Leipzig, 1835–1838.
Athenaeus. The Deipnosophists. Edited by C. B. Gulick. 7 vols. London, 1927–1928. Loeb Classical Library.
Barclay, W. Educational Ideals in the Ancient World. London, 1959.
Barry, P. "Greek Music," Musical Quarterly 5, 1919.
Becker, O. "Frühgriechische Mathematik und Musiklehre," Archiv für Musikwissenschaft 14, 1957.
—— Das mathematische Denken der Antike. Göttingen, 1957.
Beger, A. Die Würde der Musik im griechischen Alterthume. Dresden, 1839.
Behn, F. Musikleben im Altertum und frühen Mittelalter. Stuttgart, 1954.
Bellaigue, C. "Les idées musicales d'Aristote," Revue des deux mondes 73, 1943.
Bellermann, F., ed. Scriptio de musica. Berlin, 1841.
Belling, K. J. "Plato's Position with Reference to Art, and in Particular to Music," Music 1, 1891–92.
Belvianes, M. Sociologie de la musique. Paris, 1951.
Bénard, C. L'esthétique d'Aristote. Paris, 1887.

Bethe, E. "Die griechische Tragödie und die Musik," Neue Jahrbücher für das klassische Altertum 10, 1907.

Bignami, E. La poetica di Aristotele e il concetto dell'arte presso gli antichi. Florence, 1932.

Boeckh, A. "Über die Bildung der Weltseele im 'Timäos' des Platon," in Vol. III of his Gesammelte kleine Schriften. Leipzig, 1866.

Boethius. De institutione arithmetica; De institutione musica. Edited by G. Friedlein. Leipzig, 1867.

Böhme, R. Orpheus: Das Alter des Kitharoden. Berlin, 1953.

Bonitz, H. Index Aristotelicus. Berlin, 1870.

Boussoulas, N. I. L'être et la composition des mixtes dans le "Philèbe" de Platon. Paris, 1952.

Bowra, C. M. Greek Lyric Poetry, from Alcman to Simonides. Oxford, 1936.

Boyancé, P. Le culte des Muses chez les philosophes grecs. Paris, 1937.

—— "Les Muses et l'harmonie des sphères," Mélanges dédiés à la mémoire de Félix Grat. Vol. I. Paris, 1946.

—— "Note sur la tetractys," Antiquité classique 20, 1951.

—— "Sur les oracles de la Pythie: II. Les Muses, le 'pneuma' et la 'tetraktys' pythagoricienne à Delphes," Revue des études anciennes 40, 1938.

Bradley, R. H. "Aristotle's Views on Music, and Their Relation to Modern Ideas," Westminster Review 179, 1913.

Bréhier, É. Histoire de la philosophie. Vol. I, part 1. Paris, 1926.

Brownson, C. L. Plato's Studies and Criticisms of the Poets. Boston, 1920.

Brumbaugh, R. S. Plato's Mathematical Imagination. Bloomington, Ind., 1954.

Buecheler, F. "Hoi peri Damona," Rheinisches Museum 40, 1885.

Bukofzer, M. Zur Hygiene der Tonansatzes unter Berücksichtigung moderner und alter Gesangsmethoden. Berlin, 1904.

Burnet, J. Early Greek Philosophy. 4th ed. London, 1930.

—— Greek Philosophy. Part I: Thales to Plato. London, 1928.

Bury, J. B. History of Greece. 3d ed. London, 1951.

Bury, R. G. "Theory of Education in Plato's Laws," Revue des études grecques 50, 1937.

Busse, A. "Zur Musikästhetik des Aristoteles," Rheinisches Museum 77, 1928.

Butcher, S. H. Aristotle's Theory of Poetry and Fine Arts. New York, 1951.

The Cambridge Ancient History. Vols. IV–VI. Cambridge, 1926–1927.

Cameron, A. The Pythagorean Background of the Theory of Recollection. Menasha, Wisc., 1938.

Cassirer, E. "Eidos und Eidolon: Das Problem des Schönen und der Kunst in Platons Dialogen," Vorträge der Bibliothek Warburg 1, 1922–23.

Chaignet, A. E. Pythagore et la philosophie pythagoricienne. 2 vols. Paris, 1873.

Chailley, J. Formation et transformation du langage musical. Paris, 1956.

—— "L'hexatonique grec d'après Nicomaque," Revue des études grecques 69, 1956.

—— "Le mythe des modes grecs," Acta musicologica 28, 1956.

Cherniss, H. F. Aristotle's Criticism of Plato and the Academy. Baltimore, 1944.

—— Aristotle's Criticism of Presocratic Philosophy. Baltimore, 1935.

—— "Plato (1950–1957)," Lustrum 4–5, 1959–60.

—— The Riddle of the Early Academy. New York, 1962.

Chiodaroli, G. "Forma musicale e forma plastica," Acme 6, 1953.

Clements, E. "The Interpretation of Greek Music: An Addendum," Journal of Hellenic Studies 56, 1936.

Combarieu, J. La musique et la magie. Paris, 1909.

Conradt, C. Die Grundlagen der griechischen Orchestik und Rhythmik. (Gymnasial-Programm) Greifenberg, 1909.

Cooper, L. The Poetics of Aristotle: Its Meaning and Influence. Boston, 1923.

Cornford, F. M. "Mysticism and Science in the Pythagorean Tradition," Classical Quarterly 16–17, 1922–23.

—— Plato and Parmenides. New York, 1957.

—— Plato's Cosmology. New York, 1937.

—— Principium Sapientiae: The Origins of Greek Philosophical Thought. Cambridge, 1952.

—— From Religion to Philosophy. London, 1912.

Croiset, M. "Les Perses de Timothée," Revue des études grecques 16, 1903.

Croissant, J. Aristote et les mystères. Liége, 1932.

Crönert, W. "Die Hibehrede über die Musik," Hermes 44, 1909.

Curtis, J. "The Double Flutes," Journal of Hellenic Studies 34, 1914.
—— "Greek Music," Journal of Hellenic Studies 33, 1913.
Dale, A. M. "Greek Metric 1936–1957," Lustrum 2, 1957.
—— The Lyric Metres of Greek Drama. Cambridge, 1948.
—— "The Metrical Units of Greek Lyric Verse," Classical Quarterly 44–45, 1950–51.
Dantu, G. L'éducation d'après Platon. Paris, 1907.
Darak, A. Aesthetics of Music: Early Greek Views. Ann Arbor, Mich., 1951 (typescript dissertation).
Delatte, A. Les conceptions de l'enthusiasme chez les philosophes présocratiques. Paris, 1934.
—— Études sur la littérature pythagoricienne. Paris, 1915.
—— "Les harmonies dans l'embryologie hippocratique," Mélanges Paul Thomas. Bruges, 1930.
Denkinger, M. "L'enigme du nombre de Platon et la loi des dispositifs de M. Diès," Revue des études grecques 68, 1955.
Denniston, J. D. "Lyric Iambics in Greek Drama," Greek Poetry and Life: Essays Presented to Gilbert Murray. Oxford, 1936.
—— "Metre," Oxford Classical Dictionary. Oxford, 1949.
—— "Some Recent Theories of the Greek Modes," Classical Quarterly 7, 1913.
Dictionnaire des antiquités grecs et romaines. Edited by C. V. Daremberg and E. Saglio. 5 vols. Paris, 1873–1917. Includes the articles "Lyra," "Musica," and "Tibia," by T. Reinach.
Diehl, E. "Fuerunt ante Homerum poetae," Rheinisches Museum 89, 1940.
Diels, H., ed. Doxographi Graeci. 3d ed. Berlin, 1958.
—— Poetarum philosophorum fragmenta. Berlin, 1901.
Diels, H. and W. Kranz, eds. Die Fragmente der Vorsokratiker. 8th ed. 3 vols. Berlin, 1956–1959.
Diogenes Laertius. Edited by R. D. Hicks. 2 vols. London, 1950. Loeb Classical Library.
Dirlmeier, F. "Katharsis pathematon," Hermes 75, 1940.
—— "Die Oikeiosis-Lehre Theophrasts," Philologus Supplementband 30, 1937.
Dodds, E. R. The Greeks and the Irrational. Berkeley, 1956.
Döring, A. Die Kunstlehre des Aristoteles. Jena, 1876.
Dreyer, J. L. E. A History of Astronomy from Thales to Kepler. 2d ed. New York, 1953.

von Drieberg, F. Die griechische Musik auf ihre Grundgesetze zurück-
geführt. Berlin, 1841.

Duchemin, J. Pindare poète et prophète. Paris, 1955.

—— "Platon et l'héritage de la poésie," Revue des études grecques 68,
1955.

Duhem, P. Le système du monde. Vol. I: La cosmologie hellenique.
Paris, 1913.

Düring, I. "Greek Music: Its Fundamental Features and its Significance,"
Cahiers d'histoire mondiale 3, 1956.

—— "Ptolemaios und Porphyrios über die Musik," Göteborgs Högskolas
Arsskrift 40, 1934.

—— "Studies in Musical Terminology in Fifth Century Literature,"
Eranos 43, 1945.

d'Eichthal, E. "Nouvelles observations sur les problèmes musicaux attribués à Aristote," Revue des études grecques 13, 1900.

Eitrem, S., L. Amundsen, and R. P. Winnington-Ingram. "Fragments of
Unknown Greek Tragic Texts with Musical Notation," Symbolae
Osloenses 31, 1955.

Else, G. F. " 'Imitation' in the Fifth Century," Classical Philology 53,
1958.

Emmanuel, M. "Grèce," Encyclopédie de la musique. Part I, Vol. 1.
Edited by A. Lavignac. Paris, 1913.

Erckmann, F. "Sphärenmusik," Zeitschrift der internationalen Musikgesellschaft 9, 1908.

Estève, J. Les innovations musicales dans la tragédie grecque à l'époque
d'Euripide. Nîmes, 1902.

Euclid. "Sectio canonis," in Vol. VIII of his Opera omnia. Edited by
I. L. Heiberg and H. Menge. Leipzig, 1916.

—— "Section of the Canon." Translated by C. Davy in Vol. II of his
Letters upon Subjects of Literature. Bury St. Edmunds, 1787.

Fauth, W. Über Beziehungen zwischen Rhythmus, Inhalt und Aktion in
den Cantica des griechischen Dramas. Göttingen, 1953.

Fellerer, K. G. "Bericht über die Literatur zur griechischen Musik aus
den Jahren 1921–1931," Jahresbericht der klassischen Altertumswissenschaft 246, 1935.

—— "Zur Erforschung der antiken Musik im 16.–18. Jahrhundert,"
Jahrbuch der Musikbibliothek Peters für 1935.

Frank, E. "The Fundamental Opposition of Plato and Aristotle,"
American Journal of Philology 61, 1940.

—— Plato und die sogenannten Pythagoreer. 2d ed. Tübingen, 1962.

Freeman, K. Ancilla to The Pre-Socratic Philosophers. Cambridge, Mass., 1957.

—— The Pre-Socratic Philosophers. Cambridge, Mass., 1946.

Friedländer, P. Platon. 2d ed. 3 vols. Berlin, 1953–1960.

von Fritz, K. "Mathematiker und Akusmatiker bei den alten Pythagoreern," Bayerische Akademie der Wissenschaften, Philosophisch-Historische Klasse, Sitzungsbericht 1960.

—— Philosophie und sprachlicher Ausdruck bei Demokrit, Plato und Aristoteles. Leipzig, n.d.

—— "Platon, Theaetet und die antike Mathematik," Philologus 87, 1932.

Gamba, O. "Il nomos policefalo," Dioniso 6, 1938.

Gamberini, L. La parola e la musica nell'antichità. Florence, 1962. Historiae musicae cultores 15.

Georgiades, T. Der griechische Rhythmus: Musik, Reigen, Vers und Sprache. Hamburg, 1949.

—— Greek Music, Verse, and Dance. New York, 1956.

—— Musik und Rhythmus bei den Griechen. Hamburg, 1958.

Gevaert, F. A. Histoire et théorie de la musique de l'antiquité. 2 vols. Ghent, 1875–1881.

Giani, R. and C. del Grande. "Relazione melodica di strofe e antistrofe nel coro greco," Rivista di filologia classica 59, 1931.

Gigon, O. Der Ursprung der griechischen Philosophie. Basel, 1945.

Girard, J. Le sentiment religieux en Grèce d'Homère à Eschyle. Paris, 1887.

Girard, P. L'éducation athénienne au Ve et au IVe siècles avant J.-C. Paris, 1889.

Gleditsch, H. "Metrik der Griechen und Römer," Handbuch der klassischen Altertumswissenschaft, Vol. II. Edited by I. von Müller. Nördlingen, 1885.

Goblot, E. De musicae apud veteres cum philosophia coniunctione. Paris, 1898.

Goldschmidt, V. Les dialogues de Platon: Structure et méthode dialectique. Paris, 1947.

—— "La ligne de la 'République' et la classification des sciences," Revue internationale de philosophie 32, 1955.

—— Le paradigme dans la dialectique platonicienne. Paris, 1947.

Gombosi, O. J. "Key, Mode, Species," Journal of the American Musicological Society 4, 1951.

Gombosi, O. J. "New Light on Ancient Greek Music," Papers Read at the International Congress of Musicology held at New York 1939.
—— Tonarten und Stimmungen der antiken Musik. Copenhagen, 1939.
Gomperz, T. Greek Thinkers. Translated by L. Magnus and G. G. Berry. 4 vols. London, 1901–1912.
Goodell, T. D. Chapters on Greek Metric. New York, 1901.
Graf, E. "Bericht über griechische Musik von 1899–1902," Jahresbericht der klassischen Altertumswissenschaft 118, 1903.
—— De Graecorum re musica quaestionum capita duo. Marburg, 1889.
—— Der Kampf um die Musik im griechischen Altertum. (Gymnasial-Programm) Quedlinburg, 1907.
—— "Nomos orthios," Rheinisches Museum 43, 1888.
—— Rhythmus und Metrum. Marburg, 1891.
—— Die Theorie der Akustik im griechischen Altertum. (Gymnasial-Programm) Gumbinnen, 1894.
del Grande, C. "Damone metrico," Giornale italiano di filologia 1, 1948.
—— Espressione musicale dei poeti greci. Naples, 1932.
—— La metrica greca. Turin, 1960.
—— "Musica enarmonica nell antica Grecia," Rivista musicale italiana 36, 1929.
—— "Nomos citarodico," Rivista indo-greco-italica 7, 1923.
—— Sviluppo musicale dei metri greci. Naples, 1927.
Grasberger, L. Erziehung und Unterricht im klassischen Alterthum. 3 vols. Würzburg, 1864–1881.
Greene, W. C. Moira: Fate, Good, and Evil in Greek Thought. Cambridge, Mass., 1944.
Greif, F. "Études sur la musique antique," Revue des études grecques 22–24, 26, 1909–11, 1913.
Grenfell, B. P. and A. S. Hunt. The Hibeh Papyri. Vol. I. London, 1906.
—— The Oxyrhynchus Papyri. Vols. I and IV. London, 1898, 1904.
Grieser, H. Nomos: Ein Beitrag zur griechischen Musikgeschichte. Heidelberg, 1937.
van Groningen, B. A. "À propos de Terpandre," Mnemosyne ser. 4, vol. 8, 1955.
Grote, G. History of Greece. 5th ed. 10 vols. London, 1888.
Gudeman, A. Aristoteles Poetik. Berlin, 1934.
Guhrauer, H. Altgriechische Program-Musik. (Gymnasial-Programm) Wittenberg, 1904.

—— "Bericht über die Erscheinungen auf dem Gebiet der antiken Musik für die Jahre 1879 und 1880," Jahresbericht der klassischen Altertumswissenschaft 28, 1881.

—— "Bericht über die Erscheinungen auf dem Gebiete der antiken Musik von 1881–1884," Jahresbericht der klassischen Altertumswissenschaft 44, 1885.

—— Etwas von altgriechischer Musik. (Gymnasial-Programm) Wittenberg, 1909.

—— Zur Geschichte der Aulodik bei den Griechen. (Gymnasial-Programm) Waldenburg, 1879.

—— Musikgeschichtliches aus Homer. (Gymnasial-Programm) Lauban, 1886.

Guthrie, W. K. C. The Greeks and Their Gods. London, 1950.

—— A History of Greek Philosophy. Vol. I. Cambridge, 1962.

—— Orpheus and Greek Religion. London, 1935.

Handschin, J. "Die Lehre von der Sphärenharmonie," Gedenkschrift Jacques Handschin. Bern, 1957.

—— "Die Sphärenharmonie in der Geistesgeschichte," Gedenkschrift Jacques Handschin. Bern, 1957.

—— "The 'Timaeus' Scale," Musica disciplina 4, 1950.

—— Der Toncharakter: Eine Einführung in die Tonpsychologie. Zurich, 1948.

Harap, L. "Some Hellenic Ideas on Music and Character," Musical Quarterly 24, 1938.

Hardie, W. R. Res metrica. Oxford, 1920.

Harrison, J. E. Prolegomena to the Study of Greek Religion. 3d ed. Cambridge, 1922.

—— Themis: A Study of the Social Origins of Greek Religion. 2d ed. Cambridge, 1927.

Hartlaub, G. F. "Musik und Plastik bei den Griechen," Zeitschrift für Ästhetik 30, 1936.

Hasenclever, R. Die Grundzüge der esoterischen Harmonik des Altertums. Cologne, 1870.

Headlam, W. "Greek Lyric Metre," Journal of Hellenic Studies 22, 1902.

Heath, T. L. Aristarchus of Samos. Oxford, 1913.

—— Greek Astronomy. London, 1932.

—— A History of Greek Mathematics. 2 vols. Oxford, 1921.

186 *Bibliography*

Heath, T. L. Mathematics in Aristotle. Oxford, 1949.
—— The Thirteen Books of Euclid's Elements. 3 vols. Cambridge, 1908.
Heidel, W. A. "The Pythagoreans and Greek Mathematics," American Journal of Philology 61, 1940.
Heinimann, F. Nomos und Physis. Basel, 1945.
Henderson, I. "Ancient Greek Music," in Vol. I of The New Oxford History of Music. Edited by E. Wellesz. London, 1957.
—— "The Growth of Ancient Greek Music," Music Review 4, 1943.
—— "The Growth of the Greek harmoniai," Classical Quarterly 36, 1942.
Hincks, M. A. "Le Kordax dans le culte de Dionysos," Revue archéologique ser. 4, vol. 17, 1911.
Hipkins, A. J. "Dorian and Phrygian," Sammelbände der internationalen Musikgesellschaft 4, 1902–03.
Hippocrates. Edited by W. H. S. Jones. 4 vols. London, 1923–1931. Loeb Classical Library.
Höeg, C. Graesk musik: en kulturhistorisk skizze. Copenhagen, 1940.
von Hornbostel, E. M. "Tonart und Ethos," Festschrift für Johannes Wolf. Berlin, 1929.
Howald, E. "Eine vorplatonische Kunsttheorie," Hermes 54, 1919.
Huber-Abrahamowitcz, E. Das Problem der Kunst bei Platon. Basel, 1954.
Huchzermeyer, H. Aulos und Kithara in der griechischen Musik bis zum Ausgang der klassischen Zeit. Münster, 1931.
Husmann, H. "Olympos: Die Anfänge der griechischen Enharmonik," Jahrbuch der Musikbibliothek Peters für 1937.
Iamblichus. De communi mathematica scientia. Edited by N. Festa. Leipzig, 1891.
—— Protrepticos. Edited by H. Pistelli. Leipzig, 1888.
Issberner, R. "Dynamis und Thesis," Philologus 55, 1896.
Jaeger, W. Aristotle. Translated by R. Robinson. 2d ed. Oxford, 1948.
—— "Diokles von Karystos und Aristoxenos von Tarent über die Prinzipien," Hermeneia: Festschrift Otto Regenbogen. Heidelberg, 1952.
—— Paideia: The Ideals of Greek Culture. Translated by G. Highet. 3 vols. New York, 1943–1945.
Jammers, E. "Rhythmische und tonale Studien zur Musik der Antike und des Mittelalters," Archiv für Musikforschung 6, 1941.
von Jan, K. "Bericht über griechische Musik und Musiker von 1884–99," Jahresbericht der klassischen Altertumswissenschaft 104, 1900.

—— "Die Harmonie der Sphären," Philologus 52, 1893.

—— "Neue Sätze aus der Rhythmik des Aristoxenos," Berliner philologische Wochenschrift 19, 1899.

von Jan, K., ed. Musici scriptores Graeci. 2 vols. Leipzig, 1895–1899.

Janssens, A. J. "Aristoteles en de oudere muziekaesthetiek," Philologische Studien 6, 1934–35.

—— "De muziekaesthetische papyrus van Hibeh," Philologische Studien 11–12, 1939–41.

—— "De Muziekpsycholoog Damoon van Oa," Tijdschrift voor Philosophie 3, 1941.

Jeanmaire, H. Dionysos: Histoire du culte de Bacchus. Paris, 1951.

Joachim, H. H. Aristotle: The Nicomachean Ethics. Oxford, 1951.

Johnson, C. W. L. "The Motion of the Voice, he tes phones kinesis, in the Theory of Ancient Music," Transactions of the American Philological Association 30, 1899.

—— "The Motion of the Voice in Connection with Accent and Accentual Arsis and Thesis," Studies in Honour of B. L. Gildersleeve. Baltimore, 1902.

Junge, G. "Von Hippasus bis Philolaus: Das Irrationale und die geometrischen Grundbegriffe," Classica et mediaevalia 19, 1958.

—— "Die Sphären-Harmonie und die pythagoreisch-platonische Zahlenlehre," Classica et mediaevalia 9, 1947.

Jüthner, J. "Terpanders Nomen-Gliederung," Wiener Studien 14, 1892.

Kahn, C. H. Anaximander and the Origins of Greek Cosmology. New York, 1960.

Kinkeldey, O. "The Music of the Spheres," Bulletin of the American Musicological Society 11–13, 1948.

Kirk, G. S. Heraclitus: The Cosmic Fragments. Cambridge, 1954.

Kirk, G. S. and J. E. Raven. The Presocratic Philosophers. Cambridge, 1957.

Kitto, H. D. F. "Rhythm, Metre and Black Magic," Classical Review 56, 1942.

Koller, E. Musse und musische Paideia. Basel, 1956.

Koller, H. "Die dihäretische Methode," Glotta 39, 1960.

—— "Enkyklios Paideia," Glotta 34, 1955.

—— "Harmonie und Tetraktys," Museum Helveticum 16, 1959.

—— "Das kitharodische Prooimion," Philologus 100, 1956.

Koller, H. Die Mimesis in der Antike: Nachahmung, Darstellung, Ausdruck. Bern, 1954.

—— Musik und Dichtung im alten Griechenland. Bern, 1963.

—— "Die Parodie," Glotta 35, 1956.

—— "Stoicheion," Glotta 34, 1955.

Koster, W. J. W. "Quaestiones metricae," Mnemosyne ser. 3, vol. 12, 1944.

—— Rhythme en metrum bij de Grieken van Damon tot Aristoxenus. Groningen, 1940.

—— "De studiis recentibus ad rem metricam pertinentibus," Mnemosyne ser. 4, vol. 3, 1950.

—— Traité de métrique grecque. 3d ed. Leiden, 1962.

Kucharski, P. Étude sur la doctrine pythagoricienne de la Tétrade. Paris, 1952.

—— "La musique et la conception du réel dans le 'Philèbe,' " Revue philosophique 141, 1951.

—— "Le 'Philèbe' et les 'Éléments harmoniques' d'Aristoxène," Revue philosophique 149, 1959.

—— "Les principes des Pythagoriciens et la dyade de Platon," Archives de philosophie 22, 1959.

—— "Sur la théorie des couleurs et des sauveurs dans le 'De sensu' aristotélicien," Revue des études grecques 67, 1954.

Kytzler, B. "Die Weltseele und der musikalische Raum," Hermes 87, 1959.

Laloy, L. "Anciennes gammes enharmoniques," Revue de philologie 23–24, 1899–1900.

—— Aristoxène de Tarente et la musique de l'antiquité. Paris, 1904.

—— "Un passage d'Euclide mal interprété," Revue de philologie 24, 1900.

Langloys, Y. L'éducation des enfants par la musique d'après Platon. 2d ed. Paris, 1914.

Laroche, E. Histoire de la racine nem- en grec ancien (nemo, nemesis, nomos, nomizo). Paris, 1949.

Lehmann, G. Theorie und Geschichte der griechischen Harmonik in der Darstellung durch August Boeckh. Würzburg, 1935.

Lienhard, M. K. Zur Entstehung und Geschichte von Aristoteles' Poetik. Zurich, 1950.

Lodge, R. C. Plato's Theory of Art. London, 1953.

Lohmann, J. "Die griechische Musik als mathematische Form," Archiv für Musikwissenschaft 14, 1957.

—— "Der Ursprung der Musik," Archiv für Musikwissenschaft 16, 1959.

Maas, P. Griechische Metrik. Leipzig, 1929.

Mansion, A. Introduction à la physique aristotélicienne. 2d ed. Louvain, 1946.

Mariétan, J. Problème de la classification des sciences d'Aristote à St-Thomas. Paris, 1901.

Marlow, A. N. "Orpheus in Ancient Literature," Music and Letters 35, 1954.

Marnold, J. "Les fondements naturels de la musique grecque antique," Sammelbände der internationalen Musikgesellschaft 10, 1908–09.

Marrou, H. I. A History of Education in Antiquity. Translated by G. Lamb. New York, 1956.

—— "Melographia," Antiquité classique 15, 1946.

—— Mousikos Aner. Grenoble, 1937.

—— Saint Augustin et la fin de la culture antique. Paris, 1938.

Martianus Capella. De nuptiis Philologiae et Mercurii. Edited by A. Dick. Leipzig, 1866.

Martin, É. Essai sur les rhythmes de la chanson grecque antique. Paris, 1953.

—— Trois documents de musique grecque. Paris, 1953.

Martin, T. H. Études sur le Timée de Platon. 2 vols. Paris, 1841.

Marx, F. "Musik aus der griechischen Tragödie," Rheinisches Museum 82, 1933.

Meibom, M., ed. Antiquae musicae auctores septem. 2 vols. Amsterdam, 1652.

Meinecke, B. "Music and Medicine in Classical Antiquity," Music and Medicine. Edited by D. M. Schullian and M. Schoen. New York, 1948.

Merlan, P. From Platonism to Neoplatonism. The Hague, 1953.

Meyer, B. Armonia: Bedeutungsgeschichte des Wortes von Homer bis Aristoteles. Zurich, 1932.

Meyer, K. "Griechische Musik," Sinica 2, 1927.

Michel, P. H. De Pythagore à Euclide. Paris, 1950.

Moberg, C. A. "Sfärernas harmoni," Svensk tidskrift for musikforskning 19, 1937.

Möhler, A. Geschichte der alten und mittelalterlichen Musik. 2d ed. Leipzig, 1907.

Monro, D. B. The Modes of Ancient Greek Music. Oxford, 1894.

Moraux, P. "La 'mimesis' dans les théories anciennes de la danse, de la musique et de la poésie," Études classiques 23, 1955.

Moreau, J. L'âme du monde de Platon aux Stoïciens. Paris, 1939.

—— La construction de l'idéalisme platonicien. Paris, 1939.

Morrison, J. S. "The Origins of Plato's Philosopher-Statesman," Classical Quarterly 52, 1958.

Moulinier, L. Orphée et l'orphisme à l'époque classique. Paris, 1955.

Mountford, J. F. "Greek Music and its Relation to Modern Times," Journal of Hellenic Studies 40, 1920.

—— "The Musical Scales of Plato's Republic," Classical Quarterly 17, 1923.

Mountford, J. F. and R. P. Winnington-Ingram. "Music," Oxford Classical Dictionary. Oxford, 1949.

Moutsopoulos, E. La musique dans l'oeuvre de Platon. Paris, 1959.

Mullach, F. W. A., ed. Fragmenta philosophorum graecorum. 3 vols. Paris, 1860–1861.

Die Musik in Geschichte und Gegenwart. Edited by F. Blume. Kassel, 1949ff. Contains articles on "Aristoteles," by U. Fleischer and W. Vetter, "Aristoxenos," by W. Vetter, "Ethos," by W. Vetter, "Griechenland," by W. Vetter and M. Wegner, "Harmonie," by H. Hüschen, and "Platon," by W. Vetter.

Neroman, M. R. La leçon de Platon. Paris, 1943.

Nesselmann, G. H. F. Geschichte der Algebra. Berlin, 1842.

Nestle, W. Vom Mythos zum Logos. 2d ed. Stuttgart, 1942.

Nettleship, R. L. The Theory of Education in Plato's Republic. London, 1947.

Neubecker, A. J. Die Bewertung der Musik bei Stoikern und Epikureern: Eine Analyse von Philodems Schrift De musica. Berlin, 1956.

Neugebauer, O. The Exact Sciences in Antiquity. 2d ed. Providence, 1957.

Newman, W. L. The Politics of Aristotle. 4 vols. Oxford, 1887–1902.

Nicomachus. Introductio arithmetica. Edited by R. Hoche. Leipzig, 1866.

—— Introduction to Arithmetic. Translated by M. L. D'Ooge. With Studies in Greek Arithmetic by F. E. Robbins and L. C. Karpinski. New York, 1926.

Niecks, F. "The Ethical Aspects of Music," Music 21–22, 1901–02.

Onians, R. B. The Origins of European Thought about the Body, the Mind, the Soul, the World, Time and Fate. Cambridge, 1951.

Otto, W. F. Die Musen und die göttliche Ursprung des Singens und Sagens. Darmstadt, 1954.

Panofsky, E. Idea: Ein Beitrag zur Begriffsgeschichte der älteren Kunsttheorie. Leipzig, 1924. Studien der Bibliothek Warburg 5.

Pasini, F. "Prolegomènes à une étude sur les sources de l'histoire musicale de l'ancienne Égypte," Sammelbände der internationalen Musikgesellschaft 9, 1907–08.

Paulys Real-Encyclopädie der classischen Altertumswissenschaft. 2d ed. Edited by G. Wissowa. Stuttgart, 1893ff. Includes articles on "Archytas," "Aristoteles," "Aristoxenos," "Damon," "Glaukos von Rhegion," "Herakleides Pontikos," "Lasos," "Metabole," "Monaulos," "Musai," "Musik," "Musikunterricht," "Nomos," "Orpheus," "Pherekrates," "Platon," and "Theophrast."

Perls, H. "Mousa: Étude sur l'esthétique de Platon," Revue philosophique 117, 1934.

—— Platon: Sa conception du Kosmos. 2 vols. Paris, 1945.

Philodemus. De musica. Edited by J. Kemke. Leipzig, 1884.

—— De muziek. Edited by D. A. van Krevelen. Hilversum, 1939.

Pianko, G. "La musica nelle commedie di Aristofane," Eos 47, 1954.

Pickard-Cambridge, A. W. The Dramatic Festivals of Athens. Oxford, 1953.

—— The Theatre of Dionysus in Athens. Oxford, 1946.

Plato. The Collected Dialogues. Edited by E. Hamilton and H. Cairns. New York, 1961.

—— The Dialogues. Translated by B. Jowett. 4th ed. 4 vols. Oxford, 1953.

—— Die echten Briefe Platons, griechisch und deutsch. Edited by E. Howald. Zurich, 1951.

—— The Epinomis. Translated by J. Harward. Oxford, 1928.

—— The Hippias major. Edited by D. Tarrant. Cambridge, 1928.

—— Oeuvres complètes. 13 vols. Paris, 1920ff. Budé edition.

—— Opera. Edited by J. Burnet. 5 vols. Oxford, 1900–1906.

—— Philebus and Epinomis. Translated by A. E. Taylor. New York, 1956.

—— The Platonic Epistles. Translated by J. Harward. Cambridge, 1932.

—— Plato's Epistles. Translated by G. R. Morrow. Indianapolis, 1962.

—— The Republic. Edited by J. Adam. 2 vols. Cambridge, 1902.

—— Republic. Translated by F. M. Cornford. Oxford, 1941.

—— Thirteen Epistles. Translated by L. A. Post. Oxford, 1925.

Plato. Works. 12 vols. Edited by H. N. Fowler and others. London, 1918–1935. Loeb Classical Library.

Pohlenz, M. "Die Anfänge der griechischen Poetik," Göttinger Nachrichten, Philosophisch-historische Klasse, 1920.

—— "To Prepon: Ein Beitrag zur Geschichte des griechischen Geistes," Göttinger Nachrichten, Philosophisch-historische Klasse, 1933.

Pöhlmann, E. Griechische Musikfragmente. Nuremberg, 1960.

Porphyry. "Kommentar zur Harmonielehre des Ptolemaios," Edited by I. Düring. Göteborgs Högskolas Arsskrift 38, 1932.

von Prantl, K. "Über die Probleme des Aristoteles," Abhandlungen der bayrischen Akademie der Wissenschaften, vol. 6, part 2, 1851.

Pseudo-Plutarch. "Concerning Music," Translated by J. Philips. In Vol. I of Plutarch, Miscellanies and Essays. 6th ed. Boston, 1898.

—— De la musique. Edited by F. Lasserre. Olten and Lausanne, 1954.

—— De la musique. Edited by H. Weil and T. Reinach. Paris, 1900.

—— Über die Musik. Edited by R. Westphal. Breslau, 1865.

Ptolemy. "Die Harmonielehre." Edited by I. Düring. Göteborgs Högskolas Arsskrift 36, 1930.

Quasten, J. Musik und Gesang in den Kulten der heidnischen Antike und christlichen Frühzeit. Münster, 1930.

Raubitschek, A. E. "Damon," Classica et mediaevalia 16, 1955.

Raven, J. E. Pythagoreans and Eleatics. Cambridge, 1948.

Rector, S. "Plato on the Education of the Young," Music 21, 1901–02.

Reese, G. Music in the Middle Ages. New York, 1940.

Regner, J. Platons Musiktheorie. Halle, 1924 (typescript dissertation).

Reidemeister, K. Das exakte Denken der Griechen. Hamburg, 1949.

Reinach, T. "La musique des sphères," Revue des études grecques 13, 1900.

—— La musique grecque. Paris, 1926.

—— "Les nouveaux fragments rhythmiques d'Aristoxène," Revue des études grecques 11, 1898.

—— "Les Perses de Timothée," Revue des études grecques 16, 1903.

Reinach, T. and E. d'Eichthal. "Notes sur les problèmes musicaux," Revue des études grecques 5, 1892.

—— "Nouvelles observations sur les problèmes musicaux attribués à Aristote," Revue des études grecques 13, 1900.

Reinkens, J. H. Aristoteles über Kunst. Vienna, 1870.

Reisch, E. De musicis Graecorum certaminibus. Vienna, 1885.

Richter, L. "Die Aufgaben der Musiklehre nach Aristoxenos und Klaudios Ptolemaios," Archiv für Musikwissenschaft 15, 1958.

Riemann, H. "Die dorische Tonart als Grundskala der griechischen Notenschrift," Sammelbände der internationalen Musikgesellschaft 4, 1902–03.

—— Handbuch der Musikgeschichte. Vol. I, Part 1. 3d ed. Edited by A. Einstein. Leipzig, 1923.

Ring, F. "Zur altgriechischen Solmisationslehre," Archiv für Musikforschung 3, 1938.

Rivaud, A. "Études platoniciennes," Revue d'histoire de la philosophie 2–3, 1928–29.

Romagnoli, E. Nel regno d'Orfeo: Studi sulla lirica e la musica greca. 2d ed. Bologna, 1953.

Roos, E. Die tragische Orchestik im Zerrbild der altattischen Komödie. Stockholm, 1951.

Roscher, W. H. Die Hippokratische Schrift Von der Siebenzahl in ihrer vierfachen Überlieferung. Paderborn, 1913.

Rossbach, A. and R. Westphal. Theorie der musischen Künste der Hellenen. 3d ed. 3 vols. Leipzig, 1885–1889.

Rostagni, A. "Aristotele e l'Aristotelismo nella storia dell' estetica," Studi italiani de filologia classica N.S. 2, 1922.

Rostovtzeff, M. A History of the Ancient World. Translated by J. D. Duff. Oxford, 1926.

Roussel, L. Le vers grec ancien: Son harmonie, ses moyens d'expression. Montpellier, 1954.

Ruelle, C. E. "Sur l'authenticité probable de la division du canon musical attribuée à Euclide," Revue des études grecques 19, 1906.

—— "Le chant gnostico-magique des sept voyelles grecques," Proceedings of the International Congress of Musicology. Paris, 1914.

—— Études sur l'ancienne musique grecque. Paris, 1875.

—— "Études sur l'ancienne musique grecque," Revue archéologique ser. 3, vol. 36, 1900.

—— "Le fragment musical d'Oxyrhynchos," Revue de philologie 29, 1905.

—— "Locus desperatus dans Aristoxène, Éléments harmoniques," Revue de philologie 30, 1906.

—— "Notice et variantes d'un manuscrit de Strasbourg contenant les éléments harmoniques d'Aristoxène," Revue de philologie 6, 1882.

—— "Le papyrus musical d'Hibeh," Revue de philologie 31, 1907.

Ruelle, C. E. "Problèmes musicaux d'Aristote," Revue des études grecques 4, 1891.

—— "La solmisation chez les anciens Grecs," Sammelbände der internationalen Musikgesellschaft 9, 1907–08.

Ruipérez, M. S. Cantidad silabica y metrica estructural en griego antiguo. Madrid, 1955.

—— "Ideas fundamentales sobre metrica griega," Estudios clasicos 1, 1952.

Ryffel, H. "Eukosmia: Ein Beitrag zur Wiederherstellung des Areopagitikos des Damon," Museum Helveticum 4, 1947.

—— Metabole politeion: Der Wandel des Staatsverfassungen. Bern, 1949.

Sachs, C. Geist und Werden der Musikinstrumente. Berlin, 1929.

—— "Die griechische Gesangsnotenschrift," Zeitschrift für Musikwissenschaft 7, 1924.

—— "Die griechische Instrumentalnotenschrift," Zeitschrift für Musikwissenschaft 6, 1923.

—— The History of Musical Instruments. New York, 1940.

—— Die Musik der Antike. Handbuch der Musikwissenschaft. Edited by E. Bücken. Wildpark-Potsdam, 1928.

—— Musik des Altertums. Breslau, 1924.

Salazar, A. La música en la cultura griega. Mexico, 1954.

—— "La música en la edad homérica," Anuario musical 6, 1951.

Sanden, H. Antike Polyphonie. Heidelberg, 1957.

Sarton, G. A History of Science. Vol. I. Cambridge, Mass., 1959.

Schaerer, R. Episteme et techne: Étude sur les notions de connaissance et d'art d'Homère à Platon. Macon, 1930.

Schäfke, R. Geschichte der Musikästhetik in Umrissen. Berlin, 1934.

Schlesinger, K. "Further Notes on Aristoxenus and Musical Intervals," Classical Quarterly 27, 1933.

—— The Greek Aulos. London, 1939.

—— "The harmoniai," Music Review 5, 1944.

—— "The Significance of Musical Instruments in the Evolution of Music," Oxford History of Music. Introductory Volume. Edited by P. C. Buck. London, 1929.

Schmid, W. and O. Stählin. Geschichte der griechischen Literatur. Part I. 5 vols. Munich 1929–1948.

Schönberger, L. Studien zum 1. Buch der Harmonik des Claudius Ptolemäus. (Gymnasial-Programm Metten) Augsburg, 1914.

Schönewolf, H. Der jungattische Dithyrambos. Giessen, 1938.

Schottländer, J. W. "Über die Anwendung der Tonalitätskreistheorie auf die Musik der orientalischen Hochkulturen und der Antike," Zeitschrift für vergleichende Musikwissenschaft 3, 1935.

Schroeder, O. Grundriss der griechischen Versgeschichte. Heidelberg, 1930.

—— "Polykephalos nomos," Hermes 39, 1904.

Schuhl, P. M. Essai sur la formation de la pensée grecque. Paris, 1933.

—— Études sur la fabulation platonicienne. Paris, 1947.

—— L'oeuvre de Platon. Paris, 1954.

—— Platon et l'art de son temps (arts plastiques). Paris, 1933.

—— "Platon et la musique de son temps," Revue international de philosophie 9, 1955.

—— "Les premières étapes de la philosophie biologique," Revue d'histoire des sciences 4, 1950.

Schünemann, G. "Ursprung und Bedeutung der Solmisation," Schulmusikalische Zeitdokumente. Leipzig, 1929.

Schweitzer, B. "Der bildende Künstler und der Begriff des Künstlerischen in der Antike: Mimesis und Phantasia," Neue Heidelberger Jahrbücher N.F. 1925.

—— Platon und die bildende Kunst des Griechen. Tübingen, 1953.

—— Xenokrates von Athen: Beiträge zur Geschichte der antiken Kunstforschung und Kunstanschauung. Halle, 1932.

Séchan, L. La danse grecque antique. Paris, 1930.

Sedgwick, W. B. "A Note on the Performance of Greek Vocal Music," Classica et mediaevalia 11, 1950.

Servien, P. "Rythme et mémoire: Un problème psychologique relatif aux mètres grecs," Revue philosophique 134, 1944.

Seydel, G. Symbolae ad doctrinae Graecorum harmonicae historiam. Leipzig, 1907.

Shellens, M. S. "Die Bedeutung der 'Katharsis' in der Musiklehre des Aristoteles," Archiv für Philosophie 7, 1957.

Shorey, P. "The Interpretation of the Timaeus," American Journal of Philology 9–10, 1888–89.

Smyth, H. W. Greek Melic Poets. London, 1906.

Snell, B. Die Ausdrücke für den Begriff des Wissens in der vorplatonischen Philosophie. Berlin, 1924.

—— The Discovery of the Mind. Cambridge, Mass., 1958.

Snell, B. Griechische Metrik. Göttingen, 1955.

Solmsen, F. Die Entwicklung der aristotelischen Logik und Rhetorik. Berlin, 1929.

Soreth, M. Der platonische Dialog Hippias Maior. Munich, 1953.

Speusippus. De Speusippi Academici scriptis. Edited by P. Lang. Bonn, 1911.

Spiegel, W. Die Bedeutung der Musik für die griechische Erziehung im klassischen Altertum. Berlin, 1910.

Stallbaum, G. Scholia critica et historica super loco Timaei Platonici de animae mundanae elementis. Leipzig, 1857.

Stenzel, J. Platon der Erzieher. Leipzig, 1928.

—— Studien zur Entwicklung der platonischen Dialektik. 2d ed. Leipzig, 1931.

—— Zahl und Gestalt bei Platon und Aristoteles. 3d ed. Bad Homburg, 1959.

Stumpf, K. "Geschichte des Consonanzbegriffes I," Abhandlungen der bayrischen Akademie der Wissenschaften, Philosophisch-philologische Klasse 21, 1897.

—— "Die pseudo-aristotelischen Probleme über Musik," Abhandlungen der preussischen Akademie der Wissenschaften, Philosophisch-historische Klasse 3, 1896.

—— Tonpsychologie. 2 vols. Leipzig, 1883–1890.

Succo, F. Rhythmischer Choral, Altarweisen und griechische Rhythmen in ihrem Wesen dargestellt. Gütersloh, 1906.

Süss, W. Ethos: Studien zur älteren griechischen Rhetorik. Leipzig, 1910.

—— "Scheinbare und wirkliche Inkongruenzen in den Dramen des Aristophanes," Rheinisches Museum für Philologie 97, 1954.

Svoboda, K. L'esthétique d'Aristote. Brno, 1927.

Tannery, P. "À propos des fragments philolaïques sur la musique," Revue de philologie 28, 1904.

—— "Du rôle de la musique grecque dans le développement de la mathématique pure," Bibliotheca mathematica 3, 1902.

—— Sciences exactes dans l'antiquité. Toulouse, 1915.

—— "Sur le spondiasme dans l'ancienne musique grecque," Revue archéologique ser. 4, vol. 17, 1911.

Tate, J. " 'Imitation' in Plato's Republic," Classical Quarterly 22, 1928.

—— "Plato and Imitation," Classical Quarterly 26, 1932.

Taylor, A. E. A Commentary on Plato's Timaeus. Oxford, 1928.

Teichmüller, G. Aristotelische Forschungen II: Aristoteles' Philosophie der Kunst. Halle, 1869.

Theon of Smyrna. Expositio rerum mathematicarum ad legendum Platonem utilium. Edited by E. Hiller. Leipzig, 1878.

Theophrastus. Metaphysics. Translated by W. D. Ross and F. H. Fobes. Oxford, 1929.

Theophrastus and the Greek Physiological Psychology before Aristotle. Edited by G. M. Stratton. London, 1917.

Thierfelder, A. "Altgriechische Musik," Sammelbände der internationalen Musikgesellschaft 7, 1905–06.

—— "Die pythagoräische Terz," Zeitschrift für Musikwissenschaft 2, 1919–20.

Thiersch, H. "Antike Bauten für Musik," Zeitschrift für Geschichte der Architektur 2, 1908–09.

von Thimus, A. Die harmonikale Symbolik des Alterthums. 2 vols. Cologne, 1868–1876.

Thomson, G. D. Aeschylus and Athens: A Study in the Social Origins of Drama. London, 1950.

—— Greek Lyric Metre. 2d ed. Cambridge, 1961.

Tiby, O. "Ancora sul nomos policefalo," Dioniso 8, 1940.

—— La musica in Grecia e a Roma. Florence, 1942.

—— "Il nomos policefalo," Dioniso 6, 1938.

—— "Note musicologiche al 'Timeo' di Platone," Dioniso 12, 1949.

Timotheus. Die Perser. Edited by U. von Wilamowitz-Moellendorff. Leipzig, 1903.

Tischer, G. Die aristotelischen Musikprobleme. Berlin, 1903.

Töpfer, K. "Die musikalische Katharsis bei Aristoteles," Zeitschrift für die österreichischen Gymnasien 62, 1911.

Torr, C. "Greek Music," Oxford History of Music. Introductory Volume. Edited by P. C. Buck. London, 1929.

Trench, F. W. "Mimesis in Aristotle's Poetics," Hermathena 23, 1933.

—— "The Place of Katharsis in Aristotle's Aesthetics," Hermathena 26, 1938.

Ulmer, K. Wahrheit, Kunst und Natur bei Aristoteles. Tübingen, 1953.

Untersteiner, M. Sofisti: Testimonianze e frammenti. Florence, 1954.

Vetter, W. Antike Musik. Munich, 1935.

—— "Die antike Musik in der Beleuchtung durch Aristoteles," Archiv für Musikforschung 1, 1935.

Vetter, W. "Zur Erforschung der antiken Musik," Festschrift Max Schneider. Halle, 1935.

—— "Die Musik im Erziehungsplane der griechischen Antike," Deutsche Musikkultur 7, 1942–43.

—— "Die Musik im platonischen Staate," Neue Jahrbücher für Wissenschaft und Jugendbildung 11, 1935.

—— "Musikalische Sinndeutung des antiken Nomos," Zeitschrift für Musikwissenschaft 17, 1935.

—— Mythos, Melos, Musica: Ausgewählte Aufsätze zur Musikgeschichte. 2 vols. Leipzig, 1957–1961.

de Vogel, C. J., ed. Greek Philosophy: A Collection of Texts. 3 vols. Leiden, 1950–1959.

Vogel, M. Die Enharmonik der Griechen. Bonn, 1959 (typescript dissertation).

—— "Harmonikale Deutung eines pythagoreischen Spruches," Festschrift Joseph Schmidt-Görg. Bonn, 1957.

—— Die Zahl Sieben in der spekulativen Musiktheorie. Bonn, 1955.

Vollgraff, G. "De lege collegii cantorum Milesii," Mnemosyne N.S. 46, 1918.

van der Waerden, B. L. "Die Harmonielehre der Pythagoreer," Hermes 78, 1943.

Walter, A. F. "Die ethisch-pädagogische Würdigung der Musik durch Plato und Aristoteles," Vierteljahrsschrift für Musikwissenschaft 6, 1890.

Weege, F. Der Tanz der Antike. Halle, 1926.

Wegner, M. Das Musikleben der Griechen. Berlin, 1949.

Wehrli, F. "Der erhabene und der schlichte Stil in der poetisch-rhetorischen Theorie der Antike," Phyllobolia für Peter von der Mühll. Edited by O. Gigon and others. Basel, 1946.

Wehrli, F., ed. Die Schule des Aristoteles. 10 vols. Basel, 1944–1959.

Wellek, A. "Das Doppelempfinden im abendländischen Altertum und Mittelalter," Archiv für die gesamte Psychologie 80, 1931.

Westphal, R. "Die Aristoxenische Rhythmuslehre," Vierteljahrsschrift für Musikwissenschaft 7, 1891.

—— Die Musik des griechischen Altertums. Leipzig, 1883.

Wheelwright, P. Heraclitus. Princeton, 1959.

von Wilamowitz-Moellendorff, U. Griechische Verskunst. Berlin, 1921.

—— Platon. 3d ed. 2 vols. Berlin, 1948.

Williams, C. F. A. The Aristoxenian Theory of Musical Rhythm. Cambridge, 1911.

—— "The Aristoxenian Theory of the Rhythmical Foot," Musical Antiquary 2, 1911.

—— "The Notes Mese and Hypate in Greek Music," Classical Review 12, 1898.

—— "The 'System' in Greek Music," Classical Review 9, 1895.

Wilson, J. C. "Musici scriptores graeci: Emendations and Discussions," Classical Review 18, 1904.

Winnington-Ingram, R. P. "Ancient Greek Music 1932–1957," Lustrum 3, 1958.

—— "Aristoxenus and the Intervals of Greek Music," Classical Quarterly 26, 1932.

—— "Greek Music (Ancient)," Grove's Dictionary of Music and Musicians. 5th ed. Edited by E. Blom. New York, 1955.

—— Mode in Ancient Greek Music. Cambridge, 1936.

—— "The Pentatonic Tuning of the Greek Lyre: A Theory Examined," Classical Quarterly 50, 1956.

—— "The Spondeion Scale," Classical Quarterly 22, 1928.

Xenocrates. Edited by R. Heinze. Leipzig, 1892.

Zeller, E. Die Philosophie der Griechen. 3 vols. Leipzig, 1919–1923.

Index

Index

92, 104, 107, 109, 132; ethical view of music and, 87-88, 89, 108-9, 114-15, 131-32; scientific study of, 140-43; order and, 147; reason and, 148-51, 161-62

Sense and Sensible Objects, On (Aristotle), 118-19

Senses, On the (Theophrastus), 165, 176*n*44

Seventeenth century, A.D., 46

Seventh century, B.C., 58

Seventh Letter (Plato), 103

Sex, 4, 12, 141

Shaman, 46

Shorey, P., cited, 168*n*22

Sicily, 12, 58, 66, 133

Simmias, 34, 36, 169*n*32

Simonides, 61

Simultaneity, 2, 3, 21. *See also* Consonance

Sirens, 20, 21, 22, 43, 45, 49

Sixth century, B.C., cosmology, 5-6; Orphism, 47; education, 59

Society, 1, 133, 137; mathematics and, 27; harmony and, 38-41; education and, 51, 56-60, 66-67, 73, 74-75, 78, 80-81, 92-95, 96, 111; Spartan, 58-59; poetry and, 64, 81; art and, 67-69, 82, 103, 163; dissolution of, 77-78, 79, 83-84; psychology and, 134; speech and, 164-65

Socrates, 19, 69, 114, 132; ethics of, 30, 32-33, 58, 63; on the soul, 36-37, 81, 117; as musician, 42-43, 50-51, 89, 113; education and, 61, 94, 111-12; Aristophanes on, 65; on grammar, 99; on beauty, 104; on Homer, 107

Solids, as elemental seeds, 25

Solon, 40, 58, 60, 61; Athenian influence of, 67

Song, *see* Voice

Sonority, 1, 11, 43, 49; abstract harmony and, 76-77, 78, 87-90, 103, 116-17; ethics and, 95, 109, 115; motion and, 98, 99, 157, 160; number and, 99-100, 154-56; scientific study of, 140, 141-43. *See also* Sound

Sophist (Plato), 23, 31, 170*n*11

Sophists, 63, 65, 106, 133; on education, 19, 61-62, 111-14

Soul: transmigration doctrine, 6-7, 36,

47; body and, 20-21, 36-38, 41, 47, 70, 72, 105, 117, 121, 124, 125, 164; justice and, 22, 69, 105; world-soul, 22-24, 26-27, 30, 108, 115; circular motion of, 23, 24, 34, 117; three parts of, 37-38, 39, 40, 72-73, 90; purification of, 47, 48, 60, 128, 163; gymnastics and, 62-63, 84; education and, 70-71, 72, 75, 76, 85, 90-91, 103, 125; musical imitation and, 74, 82, 109-10, 139; society and, 81; tuning of, 137, 154; voice and, 141, 157

Soul, On the (Aristotle), 117, 118, 119, 121, 175*nn*8-10, 13, 176*n*25

Sound: physical nature of, 16, 116-17, 139, 157-61; mathematical theory and, 154-56. *See also* Sonority

Space, 25, 88-89, 158

Sparta, 58-59, 61, 67

Specialization, 74, 85, 103, 134, 140

Spermata (seeds), 13, 25

Spheres, harmony and music of the, 88-89, 116-17

Spherics, 97-98

Sports, *see* Gymnastics

Stallbaum, G., cited, 168*n*22

Stars, 5, 15, 22, 28; in world body, 24; immortality of, 26; motion of, 117

State, The: justice and, 22, 40-41; the soul and, 69, 81, 82; education and, 78-80, 124

Statesman (Plato), 71, 72, 104, 173*n*9

Stereometry, 76, 97

Stesichorus, 61

Stoicheia, 101

"Stoicheion" (H. Koller), cited, 173*n*8

Strife, *see* Conflict

Strings, 20, 37, 109, 140; vibration of, 7, 8, 27, 154; tonal quality and, 158-59

Styles, 71-72, 73-74, 91; mixture in, 81-84, 85, 107; rhetorical, 133, 134-37; psychology and, 143-44

Sun, 5

Symmetry, 29, 33, 41, 105

Symposia, 59, 61-62, 78, 92, 94

Symposium (Plato), cited, 167*n*7, 168*n*20, 170*n*49, 171*nn*14, 19, 173*n*16; on harmony, 10, 28, 32, 35-36, 108; on philosophy, 62-63; on beauty, 104

Syrinx, 46